Marriage à la Mode

Marriage à la Mode
Three Centuries of Wedding Dress

Shelley Tobin, Sarah Pepper, Margaret Willes
Special Photography by David Garner

THE NATIONAL TRUST

First published in Great Britain in 2003 by National Trust Enterprises Ltd.,
36 Queen Anne's Gate, London SW1H 9AS

www.nationaltrust.org.uk

British Library Cataloguing in Publication Data
A Catalogue record for this book is available from the British Library

ISBN 0-7078-0358 6

Designed by Fetherstonhaugh Associates
Printed in England

Frontispiece: *Group photograph for the wedding of Sir George Johnstone Bt and Ernestine Cust, c. 1880. The bridesmaid on the right is Rosalie Chichester, who gave Arlington Court in Devon to the National Trust.*
Half-title: *A 1920s bride, from an American tally card.*

Contents

Introduction

This book concentrates on the last three centuries of wedding dress. The costume collection at Killerton House in Devon contains over sixty bridal gowns, and we have drawn from these and accompanying accessories to show how marriage clothes developed over this period. Whenever possible, we have used examples that are associated with known brides and weddings to give the social background and context. This is possible from the eighteenth century onwards; for information on earlier weddings and dress, we have to rely largely on written descriptions and portraits of royal marriages.

Anthony van Dyck painted a marriage portrait of Mary Stuart, the eldest daughter of Charles I and Henrietta Maria, and William II, Prince of Orange. This important alliance between England and Holland was solemnized in the Chapel Royal at Whitehall on 12 May 1641. The painting, now in the Rijksmuseum in Amsterdam, shows the young prince and princess (aged fifteen and ten respectively) dressed in their wedding clothes. The Prince holds his bride's left hand, indicating the wedding ring on her finger.

Surviving documents show that the Prince's richly coloured suit of velvet trimmed with silver had been made by David Juwery of London, and was finally paid for on 16 May 1641. The Princess wore a gown of silver tissue, a fine lawn collar and cuffs trimmed with needle lace, a pearl necklace, and her hair in ringlets ornamented with pearls. The jewel worn on her stomacher, a decorative shaped piece embroidered or trimmed with lace and ribbons, was a large diamond brooch given to her by the Prince the day after the ceremony. A contemporary account by Leland indicates that the youthful bride had departed with former tradition in some respects: '... her hair tyed up with Silver Ribbands, not dishevilled about her Shoulders as in former Times used'. She was accompanied by 'unmarried Ladies habited in White Satin' – seventeenth-century equivalents of bridesmaids.

The wedding suit of Mary's brother, James, Duke of York (later James II) is in the costume collection of the Victoria & Albert Museum in London. When James married Mary of Modena in 1673, he wore a wool coat embroidered with silver and silver-gilt thread, with matching breeches. The waistcoat has not survived but was possibly red, and of rich silk figured in silver to echo the decoration of the coat.

Weddings were costly affairs, just as they are today. When fifteen-year-old Isabel Maitland married Lord Elphinstone, a Scottish nobleman, on 28 April 1670, the surviving accounts for her trousseau reveal a total of over 700 Scottish pounds was paid for her 'mariadg clothes'. The value in today's money would be £4,350. This included £216 to George Gramme, merchant, for 15 ells (15^1/$_2$ yards) of 'silver table': table was a plain weave cloth, probably a mixture of silk and silver thread.

By the early years of the eighteenth century, white and silver had become firmly associated with royal weddings and with those of the nobility. The bride would be recognised by her dress, and it could be regarded as bad luck to be married in anything but white.

We have included in this book not only wedding clothes, but also descriptions of wedding flowers, food and ephemera. Formal

bouquets begin to make their appearance in the mid-nineteenth century. However, flowers have always been associated with weddings. A wonderful source for both flowers and food at a sixteenth-century wedding is provided by the *Marriage Fête at Bermondsey* painted *c.* 1570 by the Flemish miniaturist, Joris Hoefnagel, now in the collection of the Marquis of Salisbury at Hatfield House in Hertfordshire. As a miniaturist, he has shown the customs in great detail, and these support written descriptions of weddings of the period.

The bridal procession is led by two maids and two young men carrying great bride cakes like breast-plates, supported by sling napkins. Early recipe books, such as Lady Fettiplace's of 1604, refer to 'Great Cakes' which would be big enough to cut into one hundred slices. In *The Queen's Closet Open'd*, a recipe book published in 1655, specific reference is made to 'The Countess of Rutlands Receipt for making the rare Banbury Cake, which was so much praised at her Daughters (the Right Honourable the Lady Chaworths) wedding'. The cake, like Lady Fettiplace's, includes spices, ale yeast, currants, musk, ambergris and rosewater. The resulting rich fruit cake is enclosed in an outer pastry case, as seen in Hoefnagel's painting. According to the food historian,

Ivan Day, the oval shape would enable the huge cake to be manoeuvred in and out of the oven.

Following the cake bearers are two fiddlers and a bride leader bearing aloft a gilt vessel decorated with rosemary tied with little red and white 'bride knots' and bride laces of red and white ribbons with gilded flags. Rosemary features in many descriptions of Tudor and Stuart weddings, and the preacher Roger Haket explains why in a sermon of 1607: 'Another property of the rosemary is, it affects the heart. Let this rosmarinus, this flower of men, ensigne of your wisdom, love and loyaltie, be carried not only in your hands, but in your hearts and heads.'

Behind the bride leader in Hoefnagel's painting come the principal guests carrying white gloves. Gifts of gloves, along with fans, continued to be part of wedding etiquette through the centuries. Musk, ambergris and rosewater not only perfumed the bride cake, but also the gloves. In Thomas Dekker's play, *Satiromastix*, first published in 1602, unmarried ladies have arisen to strew with flowers the path from the bride's house. One teases the other for her unmarried state: 'the Silver Ewers weepe most pittiful Rosewater: five or six payre of the white innocent wedding gloves, did in my sight choose rather to be torne in peaces than to be drawne on, and

like this Rosemary (a fatall hearbe) this deade-mans nose-gay, has crept in amongst these flowers to decke th'nuisable coarse of the Brides Maydenhead.'

Flowers are not carried by the bridal guests in the painting, but they are shown strewn on the table behind, which is set for the wedding feast. Traditionally at sixteenth- and seventeenth-century weddings hippocras was drunk at the feast. This is a rich, sweetened and spiced wine, which was often flavoured with rosemary. It was drunk at the wedding of Elizabeth Stuart, daughter of James I and Anne of Denmark, to the Elector Palatine in 1613. At this very splendid royal wedding, wafers were distributed to the guests, rather than cake.

Hoefnagel does not show the bride or groom in his painting. At this period, the bride would not have been dressed in white, but in her very best apparel: the institution of the white wedding is comparatively recent. The eighteenth-century wedding dresses in the Killerton collection are in cream, blue and pink, and written descriptions make clear that these are the traditional colours. Only in the nineteenth century did the wearing of a white dress with a veil gradually become the tradition, probably influenced by the marriage of Queen Victoria, her children and grandchildren.

These fashionable white weddings were very much the preserve of wealthy families, and status could be measured in terms of fabric, lace, jewels, and the number of bridesmaids as reported in the pages of the *Queen* or the *Court Journal and Fashionable Gazette*. Their finery was echoed by the middle classes, replacing silk with muslin and wool, old lace with tulle and net, and limiting the attendants to one or two bridesmaids, appropriately dressed. Many brides, however, were married in the best they could afford, often a smart day dress which also doubled as a going-away outfit that might be worn on many occasions after the marriage.

For widows remarrying, and those grieving for recently lost relatives, attention was paid to the elaborate mourning etiquette of the nineteenth century. Black gowns were comparatively rare, but half-mourning colours such as grey and mauve were often worn.

At Killerton, as in museum costume collections, remnants of trousseaux survive. Originating as the bridal chest or 'bundle', this consisted of clothes and domestic textiles collected for the new married life. By the early twentieth century, the trousseau represented an ideal 'dozen of everything', mostly underclothes. The idea of diligently sewing linen to add to the 'bottom drawer' continued well into the mid-twentieth century, long after the practice of purchasing a complete wardrobe of clothes for married life had been discontinued. Some less well-off brides, particularly during the World Wars, when new clothing and textiles were scarce or rationed, abandoned the idea of a trousseau altogether.

In this book we have not only reproduced the wedding clothes themselves, but also included portraits, fashion plates and photographs to show how the dresses were worn and accessorised. Brief family histories have also been given where possible. One of the most poignant dresses in the Killerton collection is an inexpensive, off-the-peg day dress bought hurriedly for a civil wedding in 1943, before the groom rejoined his squadron, never to return. Although she remarried, the bride never parted with her little blue frock, and it is in tribute to her, and to others like her, that this book is written.

This book is produced to coincide with an exhibition of wedding dresses at Killerton from April to October 2003. We are very grateful to Kate Rose, Beena Ahmad and Andrew Cummins for their invaluable help in getting the book together. We would like to thank Sheila Ashby, Maureen Dillon, Jill Tobin, Margaret Trump and all at Killerton for their contributions. Thanks also to Tracey Allen, Libby Caveney and to Shaun and Sam Garner for enabling 'field trips', to Hesta Singlewood for her wedding head-dresses, and to Amoret Tanner for her help with the wedding ephemera. Last, and not least, thank you to all the brides and grooms of the past who have donated their wedding clothes to the Killerton collection, and generously shared their memories of their special day.

A WEDDING GIFT

Grand Occasions

The earliest surviving dress that is associated with a recorded wedding is in the costume collection at the Victoria & Albert Museum in London. However, it may not be the wedding dress as such. It was worn by Isabella, daughter of William Courtenay, 5th Earl of Devon, who married Dr John Andrew at Exeter Cathedral on 14 May 1744.

The dress consists of an ivory ribbed silk mantua and petticoat embroidered in coloured silks and silver thread to produce a vivid and naturalistic pattern of flowers, shells, swags and tassels. The sumptuous rococo design is worked in satin stitch and French knots, and the embroidery incorporates a variety of couched silver threads. Apart from the flat metal strip or plate, the metal was wound around a silk or linen thread known as filé (plain), frisé (frost or crinkled) or purl (coiled), depending on the treatment of the thread. These were intended to reflect the light at different points, adding a glittering three-dimensional effect to the embroidery. The dress would have been supported by side hoops which could measure as much as 1.75m/5feet in width.

This is effectively a court dress, typical of the English style of the period. Lady Alice Houblon in her memoirs of her family, describes how Miss Archer, who married Jacob Houblon in 1770, wore elegant undress for the actual wedding ceremony and put on a much more formal gown and her best jewels for the dinner held after the ceremony.

Silks and lace were labour intensive and costly to produce; imported materials and those woven with precious metal threads were even more expensive. Lady Jemima Grey's trousseau, purchased in 1723, included eighteen yards of 'rich silver and white stuff' for her wedding dress from the silk mercer John Vickers. The material cost 50 shillings a yard, a total of £45 before the dress was even made up (£3,356 in modern money). Elizabeth Ackers, her mantua-maker received just 16s (£60) for her work, showing the enormous gap between the value of the silk and the amount deemed appropriate to pay the dressmaker. Little wonder that dresses surviving from this period are often found to have been carefully unpicked and remodelled as many as thirty or forty years after they were first created.

This sample of the silk purchased by Elizabeth Parker for her wedding dress in 1751 was from the fashionable silk mercers, Hinchcliffe and Croft, of Covent Garden in London. They provided her with a fabric of complex woven design which they described as 'New flowered gro'd Gros detour Broc'd Column'. The material cost her the princely sum of 18 guineas, which in today's terms would be approximately £1,425.

A Royal Wedding: Princess Charlotte and King George III

In late summer of 1761 London was abuzz with news of two royal events: the marriage of seventeen-year-old Princess Charlotte of Mecklenburg-Strelitz to King George III on 8 September, and their subsequent coronation two weeks later. Mantua-makers and jewellers took full advantage of the fact that the trousseau was made in England to offer similar services to potential clients.

The wedding ceremony was held in the Chapel Royal of St James's Palace. Princess Charlotte wore a dress of silver tissue embroidered and trimmed with silver, with a train of violet velvet laced with gold and lined with ermine, fastened to her shoulder by enormous pearls. Horace Walpole, who witnessed the arrival of the bride with two ladies-in-waiting, described how the heavy train 'dragged itself and almost the rest of her clothes halfway down her waist'. He also noted a little tiara of diamonds and a stomacher of diamonds 'worth three score thousand pounds'.

A fortnight later, for the coronation, she wore the same gown, train and jewels: she can be seen in all her finery in Allan Ramsay's portrait in the Royal Collection. Her consort was also dazzling, dressed in a suit of gold brocade.

Snippets of Charlotte's wedding and coronation dress were saved by her

mantua-maker, Mrs Howard, and given to Emma Walker. With
the addition of board and flannel, the scraps of silk were made into
a needlecase in memory of the Queen. This is now in the
collection of the Royal Albert Memorial Museum in Exeter,
accompanied by a note 'in remembrance of the virtuous and good
Queen Charlotte'.

The Bride wore Pink

Although most references to eighteenth-century wedding dresses talk of silver and white, there are examples of other colours. The Killerton collection has three pink wedding gowns dating from the late eighteenth century, two of which are illustrated here. Pink may well have been chosen as a suitable colour for young gentlewomen.

The first dress is said by family tradition to have been worn by Alice Westcott, the daughter of an Admiral, who married during the 1770s. Although it has been altered very slightly for wear as fancy dress, the dress is a good exmple of its type; the English back or *robe à l'anglaise*, worn with a petticoat. It is made close fitting, and would have followed the lines of the stays. The material is pleated into the back and stitched down into the skirt without a waist seam. The skirt may have been worn looped up in a polonaise arrangement over the petticoat. It retains the decorative self-trimming on the neckline, made of a strip of pink silk, with pinked edges to prevent fraying. Pinking was achieved by the use of a specially shaped metal tool which stamped out the desired scalloped edge. It also meant that it was unnecessary to hem the edge of the material.

The second pink dress shown here is a 'nightgown'. This has nothing to do with

bedwear, but is a less formal day dress, usually seamed at the waist. This dress, of crisp, shiny, plain weave silk, was worn in 1793 by Marie Marguerite Françoise du Plan, aged forty when she became the second wife of John Lloyd, twenty years her senior. Marie's father, Benjamin de Ribot, Seigneur du Caila and du Plan had served in Louis XIV's army, but as a Huguenot had been forced to leave France in 1725. After years of wandering, he settled in London, where Marie was born.

The fashion plate, taken from Heidelhoff's *Gallery of Fashion*, 1795, shows how an open robe such as this would have been worn with a toning or contrasting petticoat, and a fichu at the neckline.

The Bride wore Blue

Blue was also was considered appropriate to youth: at the French court, older women who wore blue were frowned upon. Lady Alice Houblon in her family memoirs describes how a bridesmaid at a wedding in 1770 wore a robe of blue and white stripe with flowers of silver and colours, 'the soft emblem of innocency'.

A blue and silver brocade gown, possibly an earlier fabric remodelled in the 1780s, is said to have been worn for a dramatic elopement in 1786. The bride was Elizabeth Bennet, who caused a scandal by running away with the Reverend Thomas Bancroft. Her choice of blue, which represented purity and innocence, was perhaps rather inappropriate.

This dress, like the pink gowns shown earlier, would have been worn with lace, or embroidered or plain linen lawn at the sleeves and neckline in the form of a triangular folded kerchief or fichu. A similar fichu is worn by Mrs Woodley in the detail of a family portrait by Johann Zoffany. Wedding dresses such as these were smart versions of day dress, which could continue to be worn after the celebrations, rather than a special dress created for one grand occasion.

Although some brides reverted to the ancient tradition of wearing their hair down, a symbol of virginity, the bride's hair was more frequently dressed along current fashionable lines, with a linen or lace cap and ornamented with flowers or jewels depending on individual taste and finance.

In *Nollekens and His Times*, written by John Thomas Smith and published in 1778, there is a description of a bridal ensemble: 'Her beautiful auburn hair, which she never disguised by the use of powder, according to the fashion of the day, was upon this occasion arranged over a cushion made to fit the head to a considerable height, with large round curls on either side, the whole being surmounted by a small cap of point-lace, with plaited flaps to correspond with the apron and ruffles ... her shoes were composed of the same material as her dress, ornamented with silver spangles and square bristol buckles, with heels three inches and a half in height.'

The Bride wore White

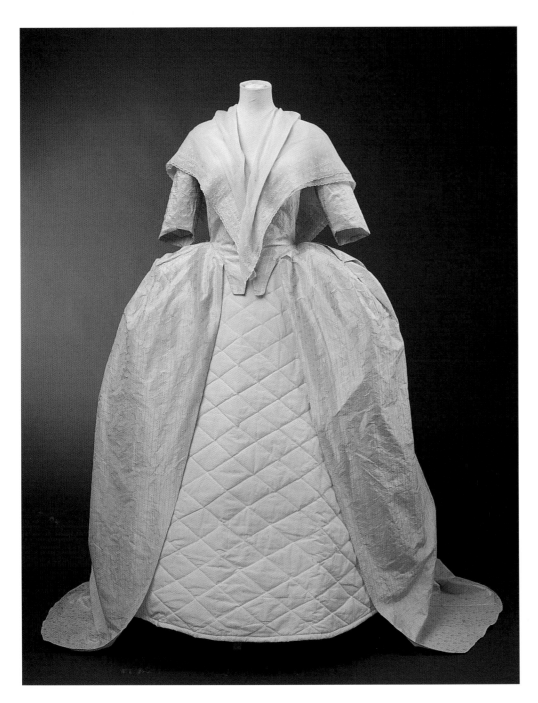

By the late eighteenth century, more frequent references are found to 'white' weddings, and indeed the superstitious thought it unwise to marry in any other colour. However, the few surviving examples are cream coloured rather than a bright optical white. A cream figured dress presented to the Killerton collection by the Hamner family of Herefordshire is said to have dressed an ancestor, Mary Dale, for her wedding to Mr Lovett in 1704, but the cut and material are of a quality and style of *c.* 1775-80.

The thin crisp silk is a finely striped taffeta with a figured design of flowers held by ribbon bows – perhaps true-lover's knots (p.58). This is an open robe, designed to be worn over a petticoat, now lost, and the width at the hips is intended to be supported by pocket hoops. There are slits in the skirt at this point to enable the wearer to reach down to manipulate the hoop or to reach her pocket, usually a flat linen bag mounted on a tape tied around the waist over the shift and petticoat.

The detail shows a back view of the bodice. The seams are covered with a decorative row of gleaming floss silk. The interior is lined with fine linen and stiffened with five whalebones at the sides and back. It fastens at the centre front with linen tapes. A stomacher may have been worn over the bodice, and corresponding

beribboned lace ruffles would have been fixed over the three-quarter sleeves, worn tight to the arm. A set of matching stomacher and a single sleeve were given with this dress, but cannot definitely be associated with the wedding. As, however, they date from *c.* 1780 and their trimmings suit the dress, it is not unreasonable to assume they are the original accessories. The stomacher is made of silk-covered linen, entirely covered with blond lace and cream silk ribbon bows. It would have been pinned into place, as would the sleeves. The surviving sleeve is not a series of dripping flounces meant to hang from the wrist, as seen earlier in the century, but made up of rows of tightly gathered blond lace, trimmed with the same silk ribbon.

An earlier dress, in blue and silver, is shown in the marriage portrait of Margaret Tyers and her husband George Rogers, painted by Francis Hayman in the 1750s, and now in the Paul Mellon Collection in the Yale Center for British Art. The presence of the cornfield and a classical urn decorated with a relief of Vestal Virgins are both symbolic.

And the Groom?

Just as most eighteenth-century brides wore smart versions of their day dress, so too did the groom. In *Pamela*, published in 1740, Samuel Richardson describes the marriage of a maidservant to a man of superior status. While she wears white flowered with silver, 'My dear Sir' wore 'a fine laced silk waistcoat, of blue Paduasoy, and his coat a pearl coloured fine cloth with gold buttons and button-holes, and lined with white silk'.

Likewise, Mary Granville in her autobiography describes her husband wearing 'a dark green coat with a very pretty waistcoat'.

Perhaps this was of embroidered silk, like the detail of a green waistcoat shown here. The waistcoat, dating from the early 1770s, has delicate tambour embroidery around the pocket flap.

In an anonymous caricature entitled 'A Fleet Wedding', published in 1747, the artist shows the bridegroom, a young sailor, fashionably dressed for the occasion. This engraving is recording the clandestine weddings performed without licence first in the chapel of the Fleet Prison, and later in other parts of London – here the ceremony is taking place at Rotherhithe. The luckless groom is duped into marrying a prostitute; her mother, a bawd, is shown stepping down from a carriage; the dénouement takes place at the wedding breakfast (pp.24-5).

Although Fleet weddings were declared void when abolished by an Act of Parliament in 1753, in his *Account of London*, Thomas Pennant describes the Fleet district as still offering this service: 'Along this lawless space was hung up the frequent sign of a male and female hand conjoined, with <u>Marriages performed within</u> written beneath.'

A FLEET WEDDING.

Between a brisk young Sailor & his Landlady's Daughter at Rederiff.

Scarce had the Coach discharg'd its trusty Fare,	Pray step this way – just to the Pen in Hand	Th'alarmed Parsons quickly hear the Din!	Till slow advancing from the Coach's Side,
But gaping Crowds surround th'amorous Pair:	The Doctor's ready there at your Command:	And haste with soothing Words t'invite 'em in.	Th'experienc'd Matron came (an artful Guide)
The busy Plyers make a mighty Stir!	This way (another cries) Sir I declare	In this Confusion jostled to and fro,	She led the way without regarding either,
And whisp'ring cry, d'ye want the Parson, Sir?	The true and ancient Register is Here :	Th'inamour'd Couple know not where to go;	And the first Parson spliced 'em both together.

Publish'd according to Act of Parliament October ÿ 20th 1747.

Price 6d
Oct. 1747

23

A Wedding Feast, 18th-century Style

Weddings are now usually followed by the breaking of the fast after the official ceremony. But in her family memoirs, Lady Alice Houblon describes a different sequence at the marriage of Miss Archer to Jacob Houblon in 1770. The guests, in elegant undress, awaited the Bride at the wedding breakfast. Arriving at eleven o'clock, Miss Archer appeared in a 'night gown of silver Muslin with silver Blond [silk lace] Hat and cap'. The bride and groom then left the house and walked 'through a Lane of Tenants and a group of servants in new rich Liveries to the Church'. When the service was over, bride cakes and wine were served in the drawing room of the house and 'pieces of wedding cake were drawn properly thro' the Wedding Ring for the dreaming of many spinsters and Bachelors.' The party then dressed for dinner, assembling at 3pm in formal dress, 'the bride looking enchanting in a very rich white and silver sack with a Hoop, a suit of very fine Point lace and all her diamonds'.

The ritual of passing a small piece of cake through a wedding ring was a traditional one. In 'The Happy Village', a poem written in 1796, Henry Rowe refers to this, and another ritual involving throwing of stockings:

The wedding Cake now thro' the ring was led
The Stocking thrown across the Nuptial bed

A depiction of a wedding entertainment comes as the pendant to the caricature of the Fleet Wedding, published in 1747 (p.23). Having gone through the 'wedding ceremony', the bridal party has repaired to a tavern where they are all eating and drinking. Sailors, the parson, the mother-in-law bawd and the rest of the guests enjoy the punch and other delights, when the creditor and two bailiffs arrive to arrest the hapless groom for his wife's debts.

25

A Regency Bride

In 1812, the *Ipswich Journal* reported: 'The bride wore a robe of real Brussels point lace over white satin... . A cottage bonnet of Brussels lace with two ostrich feathers; she wore a deep lace veil and white satin pelisse trimmed with swansdown.'

The pelisse was a full-length fitted coat, worn over a matching gown, or sometimes it took the form of a coat dress. When Mary Dunham married John Anthony at Chalfont St Giles in Buckinghamshire in 1814, she wore a cream silk taffeta pelisse with matching cap.

Mary's dress has not survived, and her pelisse, which was given to the Killerton collection by the distinguished costume historian, Nancy Bradfield, is now in such a fragile condition that it could not be photographed on a dummy. We have therefore reproduced the drawing made by Nancy Bradfield. The high-waisted pelisse has a fine ribbon sash with covered button detail. The sleeves, ruched in three places with bands of chenille embroidery, are artfully made to resemble Tudor slashing, with aerophane, a silk gauze, inserted into the satin with soft gathers. The effect can be seen in a fashion plate of a walking dress in Ackermann's *Repository*, 1814.

The pelisse is decorated around the hem with chenille bobbles, known as ball fringe, and embroidered around the hem, front openings and neckline in cream chenille thread in a simple, floral design.

The centre of each flower has insertions of two-twist bobbin net.

The net was very much a novelty as John Heathcoat had only patented the bobbin net machine in 1809. In the face of violent opposition from his workers, Heathcoat and some of his staff moved from Loughborough in Leicestershire to Tiverton in Devon in 1816. At first it was not possible to produce more than a few inches of net by machine, but Heathcoat's invention was to lead to developments in technology that made it possible to produce fine imitations of hand-made laces by the mid-nineteenth century.

Fine Lace

The pelisse continued to be popular into the 1820s. Another beautiful example shown here is a pelisse-robe made in 1825 for the marriage of Anna Maria Draycott Denys to Sir Francis Shuckburgh Bt. It survives with the original Brussels lace worn as a bonnet veil.

The pelisse does not have a continuous front opening, like a coat, but opens three quarters of the way down at the centre front. It is made in a soft oyster twilled silk, trimmed with satin rouleaux and 'Van Dyck' points which emphasise the large sleeves, puffed at the head of the shoulders. Fashion has a tendency to recall historical styles, and at this period was inspired by decorative detail of the fifteenth, sixteenth and seventeenth centuries.

Gowns such as this were often weighted at the hem with thick sheep's wool wadding to support decorative puffs and 'bouillons'. The full sleeves may have been worn over padded or whale-boned sleeve puffs to support them.

According to a family letter, the lace was ordered from Haywards of London for the enormous sum of £500: the equivalent cost today would be £17,000. The letter indicates that a pelisse was not the first choice – in fact, the lace had originally been intended to make the bridal gown.

Fashion journals in the first half of the nineteenth century often refer to

Continental, and especially French blond (silk) and Brussels lace, generally regarded as the finest available. Alençon and Brussels point lace – more correctly, bobbin lace – seems to have been particularly associated with wedding dresses.

Brussels had been an important lace-making centre since the seventeenth century, producing needlepoints, bobbin and mixed laces. Alençon derives from the town in Normandy, famous in the eighteenth century for a distinctive and very costly type of lace. Production died out in the Revolution, but was revived by Napoleon I, who also sponsored revivals of the trade in Chantilly. When trade with France resumed after the Napoleonic wars, the new, delicate products of Alençon and Chantilly must have made a refreshing change from the discreet linen laces so popular at the turn of the century.

A December Wedding

Mary Elizabeth Williams married George Hammond Lucy on 2 December 1823. Not only does the wedding dress survive, but also Mary Elizabeth's account of the whole event, as written in her memoirs.

They were married at St Asaph's Cathedral near her home, Bodelwyddan in North Wales. She wore a dress of white satin with beautiful applied decoration of vine leaves and bunches of grapes on the bodice. The puffed sleeves have elaborate overlapping crescents of silk outlined with sewn piping.

Mary Elizabeth recalled the moment she dressed for the ceremony, in her memoirs written more than sixty years later: 'I fancy that I see that dear old Nurse with trembling hands and tears dimming her eyes, dressing me ... in my bridal robe of snow-white silk which she entreated she might do, and then standing by to watch my new lady's maid, Turner, arrange my hair and the wreath of orange blossoms, with the lace veil of texture fine as a spider's web falling over all.' This veil, of exquisite Brussels lace, had been a present from her future husband.

The fine silk of the dress is now in a very delicate condition, appearing more cream coloured than the snow white described. The puffed Tudor-style sleeves recall the pelisse worn by Anna Maria (p.28), while the rouleaux trimming and

the vine leaf and grape decoration are typical of fashionable dress of the early 1820s, and are similar to descriptions in contemporary journals such as Ackermann's *Repository*.

After the ceremony, Mary put on a 'large swan's down tippet which reached to my feet, with my hands in a muff of swan's down large enough for a harlequin to jump through'.

This Regency wedding appears to have had all the trappings now associated with traditional bridal customs. The attendants were Mary's four sisters and two friends, dressed in white cashmere, their bonnets lined with pink, Mary Elizabeth's favourite colour.

Her bridesmaids threw old satin shoes for luck, and the carriage in which the bridal couple left for their honeymoon was 'decked out with large white favours'.

Two weeks later, after a honeymoon in London, George took his bride home to his beautiful but run-down Tudor mansion, Charlecote Park in Warwickshire. Mary Elizabeth's first reaction was 'so cold – oh the cold!'.

The portrait bust of Mary Elizabeth was made in 1830 by William Behnes.

A Royal Wedding: Queen Victoria and Prince Albert

Queen Victoria married her cousin, Prince Albert of Saxe-Coburg, in the Chapel Royal at St James's Palace on 10 February 1840. Sir George Hayter produced a painting of the ceremony from which engravings were made and published, thus communicating court taste to a wide audience.

In her diary, the Queen described dressing for the wedding: 'I wore a white satin gown with a very deep flounce of Honiton lace, imitation of old. I wore my Turkish diamond necklace and earrings, and Albert's beautiful sapphire brooch.'

In a departure from the state robes worn by previous monarchs, Victoria's creamy white, Spitalfields silk satin gown followed contemporary fashionable taste and was cut on simple lines, with a deep 'v' at the waist and a low, wide neckline. All seams were piped, as usual for the time, and the short full sleeves were prettily gathered into puffs. Even *The Times* commented on its simplicity.

The 65-mm ($25^1/_2$-in) deep, rich flounce of lace on the skirt, the ruffled sleeves and bertha collar were reminiscent of seventeenth-century dress. A long satin train, reportedly six yards (approx two metres) long and trimmed with sprays of orange blossom, was attached at the waist. This was carried by her twelve attendants, as can be seen in a hand-painted lithograph 'bioscope' that was produced by William Spooner of London to commemorate the event.

One of her attendants, Lady Wilhelmina Stanhope, wrote later of their experience, for the train was 'rather too short for the number of young ladies who carried it. We were all huddled

Guard Room.

Master of the Horse.   Lady E. C. Paget.   Lady Mary Grimston. Lady E. West.   Lady F. Cowper.   Lady S. Villiers   Lady A. Paget.   The Queen.   Vice Chamberlain, Sword
Earl of Albemarle.   Lady Mary C. Howard. Lady H. Bouverie.   Lady C.L.W. Stanhope. Lady Ida Hay.   Lady E. Howard.   Lady C. A. Gordon Lennox   Earl of Belfast.   Visc
Melbo

together, and scrambled rather than walked along, kicking each other's heels and treading on each other's gowns.'

The Queen's hair was fashionably dressed, smoothly, neatly and close to the head, a circlet of orange blossom around the crown, over which was placed a veil of the same lace as the dress garniture. In a desire to boost the depressed domestic lace industry, a design was commissioned from the pre-Raphaelite painter and director of the Government School of Design, William Dyce. It was then entrusted to Jane Bidney who supervised the Devon lacemakers. According to the *Windsor and Eton Express*, 'The lace intended for her Majesty's bridal dress, though popularly called Honiton lace, was really worked at the village of Beer, which is situated near the sea-coast, about ten miles from Honiton.'

Lace of this quality had long been regarded as an investment to be passed on to future generations, and Victoria was no exception to this rule. The Queen wore her wedding lace at subsequent royal marriages, and her youngest daughter, Princess Beatrice, wore it as her wedding dress in 1885.

The Coming of the Crinoline

By the 1850s, the fashion plate bride frequently appeared in a cloud of white as fashion dictated that skirts become fuller. At first, the distended skirts were displayed over layers of petticoats, sometimes stiffened with cording or aided by a horsehair 'crinoline'. From the mid-1850s a new form of petticoat was available in the form of a hooped underskirt constructed from cotton or linen and whalebone or fine wires. Despite contemporary ridicule and repeated predictions of its demise, the fashion for the artificial crinoline persisted for over twenty years.

Not surprisingly, elements of eighteenth-century dress were revived in the form of elegant ruffles and silk brocades. Waists appeared smaller, and the silhouette was balanced with large sleeves, from the full, wide pagoda to a closed bishop's sleeve. The fashion plate from the *Ladies Companion* of June 1857 shows a bride on the left. Her veil is worn low on the back of the head and pinned over the head-dress of pendant sprays of blossom, so that it could be thrown back after the wedding ceremony to create a double fall of tulle at the back of the dress. Because of the width of the material required to make the crinoline skirts, dresses were now made in two pieces. Some bridal gowns were provided with two bodices, a day style and a short sleeved evening style, thus prolonging the use of the ensemble.

Some brides preferred to wear a wedding bonnet rather than a veil, and this was equipped with its own bonnet veil attached to the crown of the millinery.

When the celebrated author, Charlotte Brontë, married her father's curate, Arthur Bell Nicholls on 29 June 1854, she wore a bonnet and veil. As a bride aged thirty-eight, a wedding veil and wreath would have been considered inappropriate. But the bonnet is extremely pretty and delicate; the milliner has added cream silk ribbon to the fragile blond lace, and the brim is trimmed with a spray of artificial flowers and feathers. Sadly, the marriage was short-lived, as Charlotte died during pregnancy the following year.

Her wedding bonnet, along with her going away dress, is preserved by the Brontë Parson Museum in Haworth in Yorkshire.

A Lace-maker's Wedding

This crinoline wedding dress was worn by Mary Tucker from Branscombe on the East Devon coast. She was the eldest daughter of a prominent lace dealer and manufacturer, John Tucker, who supplied Princess Alexandra's wedding lace when she married the Prince of Wales in 1863 (p.46).

At the age of twenty-eight, Mary Tucker married John Ford on 6 December 1864. Her plain ivory silk taffeta gown was fitted and made at Mary's home by Miss Bromfield, a local dressmaker. The simple neat bodice and wide skirt with fullness at the back was in accord with the latest taste, as shown in the fashion plate. The lack of ornament served as a foil for the veil, which Mary is said to have designed herself.

The veil is composed of a fine white machine net, decorated with Honiton pillow-made lace motifs invisibly sewn to the foundation. The lace-making areas of East Devon, centred in Honiton, had produced some of the finest laces from the seventeenth century onwards. The lace was worked on pillows with bone or wooden bobbins: this mainly cottage-based industry suffered at the end of the eighteenth century when possibly half the market was lost as changing tastes in fashion decreed that both men and women wear more discreet trimmings. In

addition, the 'twist-net fever' resulting from the expiry of John Heathcoat's patent (p.26) flooded the market with machine-made net.

However, help was at hand. The royal family provided strong and enduring support for the Devon lace industry. Queen Victoria, her daughters, the Princess Royal and Princess Louisa, and her daughter-in-law, Princess Alexandra, all wore Honiton lace for their weddings. Ironically, the availability of machine net also eventually helped to boost the trade by providing a foundation to which the pillow-made motifs could be applied, as with Mary Tucker's veil.

A Marriage in High Life

'If I had the tongue or pen ... I should give you quite a vivid, and at the same time refined, description of that edifying spectacle – a marriage in high life. How eloquent, and by turn pathetic and humorous, I could be on the bevy of youthful bridesmaids – all in white tulle over pink glacé silk, all in bonnets trimmed with white roses ... . How I could expatiate, likewise, on the appearance of the beauteous ... bride, her Honiton lace veil, her innumerable flounces; and her noble parents, and the gallant and distinguished bridegroom.' G.A.Sala's *Twice Round the Clock; or the Hours of the Day and Night in London*, written in 1859, provided the artist George Elgar Hicks with the inspiration for 'Changing Homes', painted in 1862.

The painting, which now hangs in the Geffrye Museum in London, shows a wedding party on their return from church. Within the opulent drawing room, all the details of a Victorian wedding may be glimpsed. On the right, a bridesmaid tries to prevent her brother from grabbing and breaking one of the ornate wedding presents set out on a table. More bridesmaids with baskets of flowers are shown on the left. The bride has a white lace crinoline dress similar to that worn by Princess Alice, second daughter of Queen Victoria and Prince Albert, when she married Prince Louis of Hesse at Osborne House in 1862. Royal weddings led the fashion, and Hicks would have seen illustrations of the dress in magazines.

The bridegroom wears a black coat and grey brown trousers with a waistcoat. This is similar to one of 'white quilting' recommended for bridegrooms in Minister's *Gazette of Fashion* of 1861. The lady on the right of the bride, possibly her mother, is wearing a splendid mauve dress, one of the brave new colours produced as a result of William Perkins' experiments with aniline dyes (p.48). In the background a wedding cake with several layers, decorated with icing, may be seen.

Bridal Wreaths and Corsages

In Tudor and Stuart England, the bride might well have worn a wreath on her head: traditionally of roses, myrtle and rosemary, though sometimes of leaves of corn, often accompanied by a veil. The Georgian bride, however, rejected these in favour of a hat. Flowers, both real and artificial, made a comeback at mid-nineteenth-century weddings. The bride often wore a corsage at her waist, as can be seen in the fashion plate on p.35, or on her head as a wreath. The recreation of a Victorian corsage shown here is made up of lily of the valley, stephanotis, jasmine leaves, orange blossom and leaves, rosebuds and asparagus fern. For the head-dress, bridal gladiolus has been added.

John Philip's painting of the wedding in 1858 of the Princess Royal, eldest daughter of Victoria and Albert, to Crown Prince

Frederick of Germany shows how the bride and her bridesmaids are wearing quite large wreaths of roses on their heads. The wedding adopted a Highland theme, with the groom and the bride's brothers wearing tartan. The bride is positively awash with bouquets of artificial roses and white heather on every part of her gown.

C.T.Hinckley, writing in the *Ladies Companion* of December 1854, provides a fascinating account of the complicated manufacture of artificial flowers so indispensable to milliners and dressmakers. Although the author does not disclose the location of the workroom studied, Italy and France are mentioned as centres of the finest products. Each workroom was equipped with long tables fitted with drawers and compartments containing the minute flower parts ready for assembly. The flowers for bridal wreaths were made from 'the purest virgin wax, entirely freed from all extraneous matters'. Much care was needed in colouring the wax, 'the colours being in fine powder, are made into a paste by adding little by little of essence of citron or lavender'.

Textiles were also used, including silk, gauze, velvet, muslin and cotton cambric, to create leaves and petals before being gaufered into shape. Green silk taffeta, ready dyed in the piece, was used for leaves, but the petals and other parts were hand painted. According to Hinckley, buds were formed by padding taffeta or tinted kid with cotton or, alarmingly, 'crum of bread', and tied onto the stem with fine wire, which was then wrapped in green material.

Bridal Bouquets

The cover of sheet music for 'The Wedding Galop', composed c. 1860, shows a bride getting into her carriage en route for the church. The bouquet that she carries may well have been provided by her groom, as dictated by the etiquette of the period. The flowers have been arranged tightly in a circular bouquet – special posy holders were produced in silver, metal or straw-work, with lace to surround the flowers. The recreation shown here used white carnations, bridal gladiolus, stephanotis and asparagus fern.

In 'Changing Homes' (pp.38-9), the bride and one bridesmaid have these tight round bouquets, but the other bridesmaids in the painting carry little baskets of flowers. We have recreated a bridesmaid's basket using sweet peas, honeysuckle, spray and bud roses, roses, lily of the valley, daisies and pinks. Rosemary, the traditional herb for weddings, and myrtle are arranged around the outside of the basket so that they can give off fragrance as their leaves brush against skirts.

Later in the nineteenth century, bouquets for brides and their bridesmaids become much larger and looser, as in the recreation shown here with carnations and asparagus and leather jacket ferns.

The Wedding Cake

In the eighteenth century, icing and almond paste became traditional ingredients for wedding cakes. When the cookery writer Elisabeth Raffald published a recipe for a bride cake in *The Experienced English Housekeeper* in 1769, the dough shell of the Tudor cake (p.9) had been replaced by a paper-lined wooden hoop. After baking, the cake was covered with almond paste and then with sugar icing.

Sugar decoration, however, does not seem to have been introduced until the end of the century. In his diary for 1795, the Rev. James Woodforde records 'a large piece of fine wedding cake' being sent up to Norfolk from London, and refers to 'very curious devices on Top of the Cake'. Confectioners produced wooden moulds for making various devices in sugar paste, including figures. A tantalising mould, made of card, is in the Pinto Collection in Birmingham. Probably dating from the early eighteenth century, it would have been able to construct a three-dimensional tester bed which suggests that it was used for wedding cakes.

The encrusted wedding cake is a nineteenth-century invention. The cake for Queen Victoria's wedding to Prince Albert in 1840 was a huge confection, three yards in circumference and weighing 300 pounds. A reproduction of the cake has been used here on a baker's paper bag.

Gunter & Ward of London produced the first tiered wedding cake for the wedding of the Princess Royal in 1858. The three tiers reached a height of over six feet and were separated by rows of pearls and festooned with garlands of orange blossom, jasmine and silver leaves. Columns supported the uppermost tier, which was dome-shaped and crowned with cupids displaying likenesses of the bride and groom.

The manufacture of wedding cakes became a thriving industry. Chester was the centre for cake confectionery in England, though Thomas Wood, 'Artistic Confectioner' from Liverpool, may well have begged to differ. Cakes of the 1860s and '70s were surmounted by real flowers in a silver vase, or with artificial and frosted flowers in vases made of sugar paste. Such decoration can be seen in the cartes-de-visite dating from the 1860s. Other decorations included ribbon favours and good luck charms that could be distributed to guests. By tradition, the top layer of the cake was kept for the christening of the first child.

PLUMTREE   LOUTH

44

HER MAJESTY'S BRIDAL CAKE.

The Photographer's Studio

The development of photography provided a wonderful opportunity to capture the memories of weddings. Before, only the royal family and the richest could afford to commemorate their marriages in paintings and engravings. The first royal wedding to be photographed was that of the Princess Royal, eldest daughter of Queen Victoria and Prince Albert, who married the Crown Prince of Germany in 1858.

Five years later, on 10 March 1863, the Prince of Wales married Princess Alexandra of Denmark in St George's Chapel, Windsor. The bride's gown of silver tissue is said to have been supported by layers of petticoat since she disliked wearing a crinoline. The train was of silver moire antique, and the full skirt of the dress was trimmed with chains of orange blossom, myrtle and bouffants of tulle with Honiton lace. Her bridal veil, also of Honiton lace, was furnished by the Branscombe lace merchant, John Tucker (p.36). Again the photographer was present to record the occasion, taking not only this image of the bridal couple, but also the extraordinary picture of the Queen, swathed in black, gazing at a bust of her deceased Albert, with the bride and groom looking mournfully on.

By the 1870s, most large towns had at least one photographer's studio. Although few families could afford the photographer's

services at the wedding, surviving cartes-de-visite can be found not only of bridal couples, but also of wedding cakes (p.44). Bride and groom might be photographed separately before or soon after the wedding. Day clothes, rather than splendid bridal toilettes are often depicted, and without a firm provenance, it is difficult to distinguish the sitters as dressed in wedding clothes.

Home entertainments, such as stereoscopes, were sold with a set of photographs mounted on card. The subjects varied from pictures of the Swiss Alps to the crowned heads of Europe, and sometimes illustrated moralistic stories. The melodramatic pose of the bride in the photograph shown above right suggests that it is such a card, rather than a genuine bridal portrait. However, it does help to reinforce the image of the virgin bride which had become almost stereotypical.

W.R.Downey enjoyed the distinction of being photographer to Queen Victoria. His cabinet photograph, above left, shows the bride in full regalia, with bouffant skirt, probably tulle, caught up with orange blossom.

Brave New Colours

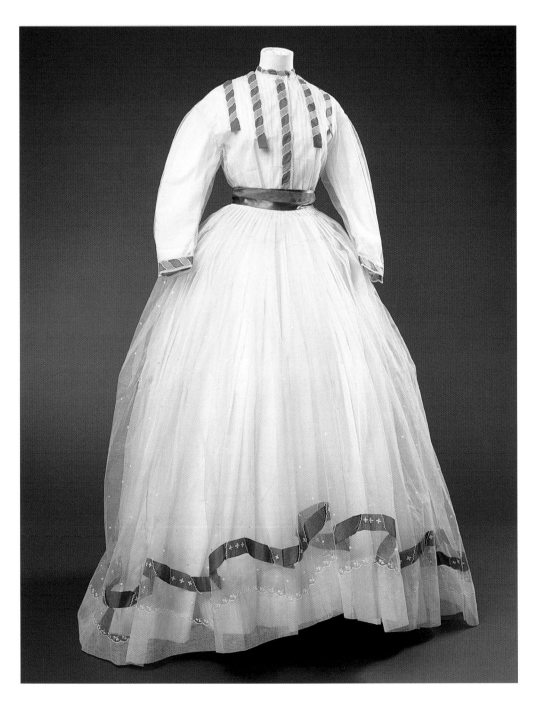

By the mid-nineteenth century, the connotations of innocence, purity and implied virginity were firmly associated with the wearing of white. If white was not worn, it could indicate that the bride was unable to afford a dress specially made for the occasion. Coloured dresses were not only more economical, as there was greater potential for future wear, but could also take advantage of the new chemical dyes developed in the 1850s after William Perkins' discovery of mauve that produced brilliant colours such as blue, magenta and pink.

Touches of bright blue can be seen on an 1860s wedding dress worn by Alice Mary when she married Charles Roberston, founder of the Royal Watercolour Society. Her husband's patented 'ready-made' blue satin cravat has also been preserved. The dress has a full, rounded crinoline skirt, high neckline and long, full bishop's sleeves. The lightly embroidered muslin is also worked with slots to take the blue ribbon. Muslins had become popular by this period because they could be trimmed to profusion.

The half century between the death of the Prince Consort in 1861 and the death of his eldest son, Edward VII in 1910, could be described as the golden age of mourning. For family mourning there was a carefully arranged system. A widow was expected to remain in mourning for two years, a parent for one, siblings and grandchildren for six months, down to second cousins for three weeks. The first period would be full mourning, when deep black clothes were worn. The second period was half mourning, when shades of grey, mauve and lilac were acceptable.

In general, stark white and half mourning colours were approved of for bereaved brides. The lilac dress, *c.* 1870, was probably for a bride in half mourning. It reflects the height of fashion for the time: towards the close of the 1860s, fashion leaders had replaced the full crinoline skirts with rounded, high-waisted dresses. The extravagant fullness at the back of these gowns was supported by a half crinoline or crinolette. By the 1870s, these were being replaced by smaller tournures, known vulgarly as bustles. This dress consists of three pieces: bodice, skirt and tablier, an apron-like overskirt. The fabric is an exquisite figured silk, with a lilac and cream sprig. The only decoration is silk fringing.

A Victorian Trousseau

For centuries would-be brides gathered together their trousseaux, outfits of clothes and linen for their new households. As we have seen, very large amounts of money could be spent on these.

By the nineteenth century, the trousseau had become a major area of discussion, and magazines were happy to provide advice, as the illustrations show. In the *Englishwoman's Domestic Magazine* of May 1862, a bride seeking to practise economy is advised: 'Marion. By reducing the number of articles in the Trousseau, and having six instead of 12 of different things, you will arrive at something suitable for your income'.

Women reserved their prettiest and most decorative underwear for their trousseaux. The *Queen* announced in 1880: 'In no item of dress has there been more changes in fashion of late years than in underwear. The chief aim now seems to be to minimise all such garments. Washing silk (both cream and coloured) has taken the place of cambric and linen for day and night chemises. White flannel petticoats are things of the past; coloured flannel, with much fancy stitching and torchon lace, has superseded them; also black satin skirts lined with chamois leather. Black satin stays are fast taking the place of white coutil, and stocking suspenders have dethroned garters.'

The elaborately frilled and embroidered trousseau items in the photograph date from the 1870s or '80s, and are in a style that is similar to embroidery patterns offered at this time by the *Queen*.

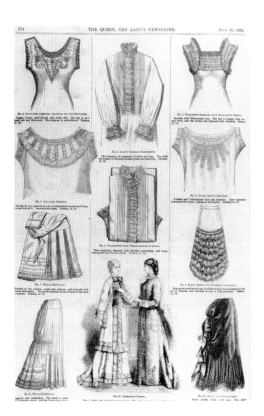

The Wedding Breakfast, Victorian Style

In the 1870s the sixteenth- and seventeenth-century practice of strewing dining tables with flowers was revived. Aesthetic tables would be decorated with artistic and random scatterings of flowers and leaves. But more conventional households could decorate their dining tables with formal tracery. John Perkins, head gardener to Lady Henniker at Thornham Hall in Suffolk, spent his retirement writing *Floral Decorations for the*

Table published in 1877. The book contains 24 detailed plans in colour of table settings for dinners, luncheons, a hunt breakfast, a cricket luncheon and Christmas.

Reproduced here is his plan for a wedding breakfast. For the lower part of the wreath he recommends myrtle with cyclamen blooms and 'pips' of white hyacinth. However, he sensibly points out that 'As interesting events, such as Weddings, are likely to take place at all seasons of the year, it is advisable that Gardeners have a good Stock of white flowering plants always in store.'

We have recreated an arrangement for one of the trumpet vases that would have adorned the table, made up of moss, snowdrops, eucharis and maidenhair fern.

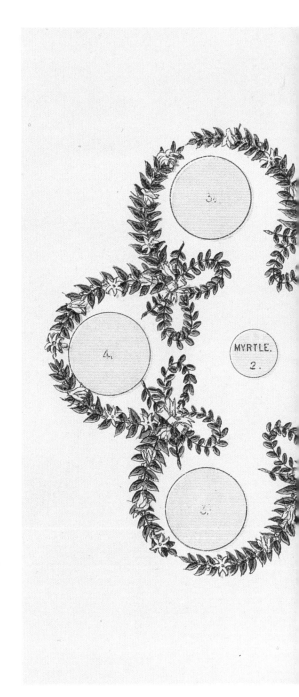

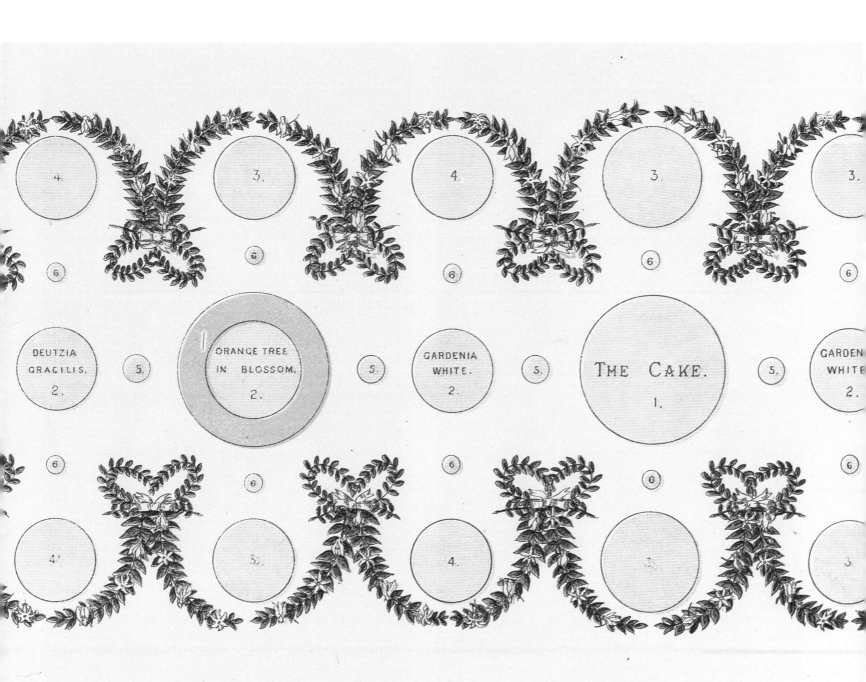

4.

3.

4.

3.

3.

6

6

6

6

DEUTZIA GRACILIS. 2.

5.

ORANGE TREE IN BLOSSOM. 2.

5.

GARDENIA WHITE. 2.

5.

THE CAKE. 1.

5.

GARDEN WHITE 2.

6

6

6

6

4.

3.

4.

3.

3.

53

A Youthful Bride

The princess line came into vogue in the late 1870s. Dresses were tightly fitted to the body, made as one piece rather than as separate bodice and skirt. Even day dresses sometimes had trains, and both the construction and the ornament of these gowns could be extremely complicated.

The fussiness and restriction of such garments led to disapproval from dress reformers. Mrs Haweis, author of *The Art of Dress* published in 1879, wrote that their wearers appeared to be 'living mummies' imprisoned in swathes and bands of silk and satin. Another observer remarked that 'simplicity is out of fashion'. 'At the present moment women go about hobbled after the fashion adopted by our forefathers to prevent the straying of their horses and asses when turned out to grass' was the acerbic view of a third commentator.

A typical wedding dress of 1880 would be made of satin with deep box pleats, perhaps with a tunic effect or pleated panniers at the hips, and elbow-length sleeves and ruffles. Veils were worn long, reaching to the ground. The dress illustrated here has a very youthful air, with its slender line and delicate mixture of rosebuds and gauze trimming to the back, neckline and sleeves. It would have been worn over a corset and the latest combination garment to minimise layers of bulky underwear.

The fine ribbed silk is offset by panels of glossy satin forming a plastron and pleated panniers at the front, and extravagant bustle drapery at the back. The bustle arrangement is further emphasised by a large grosgrain bow.

A fashion plate from the *Queen*, dated 5 February 1887, offers patterns by post for a bride's ensemble and bridesmaid's dress. The pattern for the bridal toilette is priced at 5s 7d, and for the bridesmaid's costume at 2s 7d for the bodice pattern and 3s 1d for the skirt.

The bridal outfit has fashionably asymmetrical drapery in materials suggested as follows: 'White faille Française, Alençon lace, and orange blossoms. The train has a pleating of esprit net inside its edge; the silk tablier is kilted, and covered with a lace tunic draped with orange blossoms. Bodice with folds on the right shoulder, and lace on the left.'

The proposals for the bridesmaid's costume are: 'Ivory Surah, studded with Pompadour flowers. The pente, diagonal drapery and V-shaped plastron are in heliotrope terry velvet. The collar is in lace. The waistband, of Surah, fastens in front with a bow.'

Working Brides

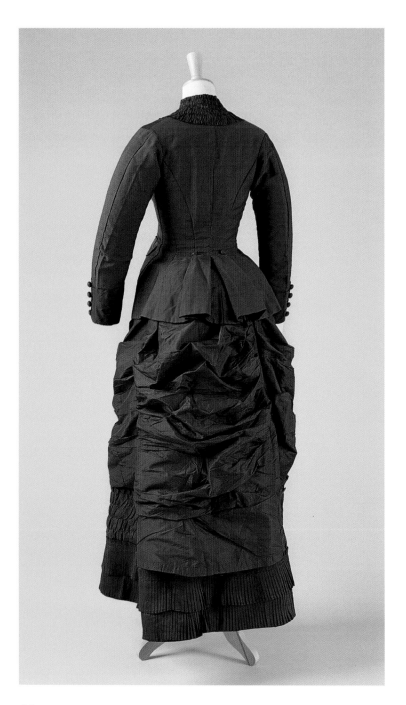

In contrast to all the glorious intricacy and richness of the society gowns were the dresses of working-class brides. Working women were advised to choose practical clothing. 'Daisy', a correspondent to the *Girl's Own Paper*, was told to eschew white, and 'get a "nun's cloth" trimmed with satin. A light shade of the colour called "London smoke", the bonnet and gloves to match, and a white bouquet.'

A dress of brown silk and wool in the Killerton collection was worn by Elizabeth, daughter of Ezekial Kyte, a Wiltshire farm labourer, for her wedding in 1883. The ensemble is probably home-made and not of the best quality material, although the bride would probably have tried to obtain the best she could afford. There is an alternative bodice trimmed with velvet, which may have been added after the wedding. It is unlikely that Elizabeth wore a veil, which would have been very expensive. Instead, she probably had a hat or bonnet similar to that worn by Lucy, a maid of all work who was photographed on her wedding day in the early 1880s.

In 1886 changes were made to the regulations for the conduct of church weddings, and from then on, afternoon ceremonies were permitted. These quickly became popular, allowing for a wedding breakfast after the service and avoiding the afternoon pause in the celebrations. Some brides therefore wore their 'going-away dress' for the marriage ceremony. A fashion correspondent wrote in 1887 'Afternoon weddings have caused a great reform; a bride is often married in her going-away dress, and a bridal dress is always high to the throat with elbow sleeves.' Lucy has followed this advice.

Emily Grace Gale, a milliner, married Walter Oakley, an accountant, at the Mint Methodist Chapel in Exeter on 15 March 1884. The bride's mother was also a milliner, her father a tailor, so they saw to it that their daughter was fittingly dressed. The outfit came from Green & Son, a respectable family in the city who described themselves as 'Silk mercers, family drapers, milliners, costumiers, dressmakers, furriers, ladies' and children's

underclothing and funeral furnishers'.

Emily's dress would have doubled as a going-away outfit, and would probably have been worn with a bonnet rather than a veil. The ensemble consists of a separate bodice and skirt in dark russet silk, the bodice front fastening with decorative buttons, the sleeves a fashionable three-quarters length trimmed with velvet to match the stand-up collar and false waistcoat, or plastron front of the bodice. The complicated skirt is constructed over its own horsehair-filled bustle pad, and has crinolette steels inserted into the lining to keep the severe bustled form. The silk is draped asymmetrically, a sartorial conceit thought to be very chic at this date.

Victorian Wedding Favours and Ephemera

At Tudor and Stuart weddings, it was the custom for wedding favours to be distributed, often by the bridesmaids. These were made up in silk with true-lover's knots, to be worn on sleeves and to decorate the bridal bed. 'True-lovers' is derived from the Old Norse, *trulofa*, meaning 'for I plight my troth'. People who were not even at the wedding might be supplied with favours, just as pieces of wedding cake are now boxed up and sent to absent friends. Victorian wedding favours were generally made up of real flowers. Mrs Humphreys, a journalist and author of a book of etiquette, *Manners for Women*, noted in her 1897 edition that the custom of real flower favours could be costly – 'no small items when the guests number hundreds, as they usually do'.

In the nineteenth century, not only were wedding favours dispensed but, with developments in printing, a whole range of ephemera was produced. Some examples can be seen here. Two of the bookmarks are of woven silk, made by Thomas Stevens. The one on the right is decorated at the bottom with a true-lover's knot. The other bookmarks are blind embossed, dating from the 1850s. One greetings card is made of paper lace, the second takes the form of a silver horseshoe. The poem 'To a Bride' is made from silk and paper lace.

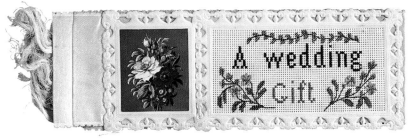

To a Bride.

When thy foot is at the altar,
When the ring hath press'd thy
    hand,
When those thou lov'st, and those
    who love thee,
Smiling round thee stand,
O, may the verse that friendship
    weaves,
Like a spirit of the air,
Be o'er thee at that moment,
For a blessing and a prayer.

Trains and Drapery

From the mid-1870s, trains became an important feature of day as well as evening dress. A description of a fashion plate from an 1876 edition of the *Young Englishwoman* conveys in great detail the characteristically complicated drapery: 'Bride's dress of white *faille* or *Sicilienne*. Trained skirt, mounted in the Bulgarian fold at the back, pleated across the front in pleats which point upwards. The *tablier* is trimmed down the middle with a *coulisse* in four rows of gathers. One of the sides is trimmed with a coquille of white lace. A double flounce of *faille* and lace terminates the *tablier*.' And so it proceeds, ending 'Wreath of orange blossom and *à la Juive* veil, falling to the lower edge of the train at the back.'

An enormous variety of hand- and machine-made lace was now available, and often used in quantity on bridal gowns. In the *Art Journal* of 1872, P.L.Simonds wrote that 'besides the enormous consumption of our cheaper Nottingham lace and the pillow-lace of Honiton, we import foreign lace to the value of more than £750,000 sterling.'

Honiton lace had survived the 'twist-net revolution'. Charlotte Treadwin, who ran a lace manufactory in Exeter from the 1860s, recalled that she knew of only one elderly lady who retained the skill to make the net ground. But now pillow-made motifs could be applied to machine-made net, and many surviving nineteenth-century veils have been produced by this technique.

The tradition initiated by Queen Victoria of supporting the Devon lace trade continued. Archive photographs from Charlotte Treadwin's records, now in the collection of the Royal Albert Memorial Museum in Exeter, refer to lace for two royal brides. The first, shown here on the left, is a border in Treadwin's own registered 'Fleurette' design, which was made to encircle a bouquet for Marie of Russia, bride to Alfred, Duke of Edinburgh, the Queen's third son, in 1874. The second, far right, was a flounce and garniture in reproduction *point d'angleterre*, made for Helena of Waldeck-Pyrmont, for her marriage in 1882 to Leopold, Duke of Albany, the Queen's fourth son.

The third piece of Honiton lace was made for a fan for the marriage of Alice Sawyer to Thomas Kennet-Were in 1876. Their arms are shown in the middle.

Sumptuous Silks

Two wedding dresses in rich ivory silk, typical of the 1880s, are in the Killerton collection. They both follow the currently fashionable line. The first (below) is a corded silk, of the *Gros de Suez* family. The tightly fitting bodice is boned and lined with cotton, and fastens with silk-covered buttons. The separate skirt is bustled, with self trimmings of pleated bands of the silk. The shoes are also shown in the photograph. These are typical of the period, of plain silk over kid to match the dress, with a small heel and self bow over the toe. More elaborate shoes might be embroidered in coloured silks or beads. The veil shown in the photograph is not associated with the dress, but representative of

a good quality Honiton appliqué veil of the second half of the nineteenth century.

The richness of the second gown (right) is achieved in the balance of silk satin and damask with lace trimming. The low decolletage is not usual. The bodice and neckline may have been altered for wear by another bride and the modesty piece lost. It was expected that a wedding dress be worn for several, if not many occasions: during the first year of marriage, the dress might remain unaltered for dinner parties, so that friends and relatives could see and admire it. During the second year, it was incorrect to wear the dress without some form of alteration to remove it from its former status. A separate court train was sometimes added, and the dress altered for the bride's first presentation at court as a married woman.

The dress is plain satin with the effect of an overskirt of rich damask, deeply pleated at the back and designed to be worn over a small, high bustle frame or pad. The hem of the train has a balayeuse frill of pleated organdie, which could easily be replaced as it acted like a carpet sweeper, catching up all the dust as the bride swept down the aisle. The front over-skirt is arranged to drape softly towards the hem, where it is caught up into lace-trimmed points over box pleats. The bodice is covered with a large piece of Honiton lace, possibly not original to the dress, since it does not match that at the hem of the skirt. The bride would have worn a full-length veil of tulle over a wreath of wax orange-blossom. Elbow-length gloves were a prerequisite with this style of dress.

A Literary Influence

The author and illustrator Kate Greenaway published nursery rhymes for children during the 1880s. Her pictures were highly influential, not least amongst designers for bridesmaid's dresses for fashionable weddings. *Marigold Garden* was published in 1885, and included the following rhyme, summing up the prettiness and romance of the ideal wedding day:

> 'The Wedding Bells'
> The Wedding Bells were ringing
> And Monday was the day
> And all the little ladies
> Were there so fresh and gay

The photograph of a wedding from the 1880s shows a group of adult bridesmaids in 'Kate Greenaway' floral bodices with peplums draped to form panniers resembling eighteenth-century dress, over tight-fitting shirred and pleated skirts. The outfits are completed by little bonnets of straw or chip (finely shaved poplar or willow woven to shape), trimmed with velvet, lace and flowers. Each bridesmaid holds a small, tightly formed posy, in keeping with those often seen in Greenaway's work.

Her influence has proved long-lived. The second wedding group, dating from 1902, shows younger bridesmaids in Greenaway-style dresses and large chip hats trimmed with lace and chiffon. The wedding was that of Nancy Mercier to the Rev.J.S.Martin at Kelmerton in Gloucestershire. The bride's dress was of ivory satin trimmed with old Chantilly lace: it is now in the Killerton collection, in fragile condition. The bridesmaids carry bunches of narcissus, the bride a sheaf of Madonna lilies.

Even today Kate Greenaway's name has come to represent a particular style of bridesmaid's dress, and especially millinery.

Weddings of the 1890s

Wedding photographs became much more common in the 1890s. Some factories and workplaces set up clubs whereby a small amount could be paid in each week to contribute to the cost of the photograph.

The photograph on the left shows the bride, Isabella or 'Bell' Adams alone in a studio setting, possibly some days before her wedding on 10 September 1898. The other, less formal photograph was taken at home in the garden with her groom and bridesmaids. The moire silk dress is in the Killerton collection. Of tiny proportions, it is significant for the extravagant stiffened Medici collar and long sash worn draped asymmetrically around the torso. Both would have served to draw attention to the bride's incredibly neat and tiny waist. The large hat, trimmed with three ostrich plumes and orange blossom, balances the whole silhouette. During the 1890s, more modish hats began to supersede bonnets, and even veils for a time.

The dress on the right was made by a North Devon dressmaker for a bride who married in Exeter Cathedral in 1894. The separate bodice and skirt are made of cream cashmere cloth. The skirt has a stiffened interlining which helps to keep the shape of the train and full A-line skirt. There is a central panel of satin at the front. The hem has an organdie balayeuse (p.62). The bodice fastens at the front with metal hooks and eyes. It is lined and boned and has the full sleeves typical of the period, covered by a cape-like fall of satin edge with fragile machine lace. The high stand collar and cuffs are bound with satin to match. Perhaps the most distinctive feature of this dress is the drapery over the hips. The photograph shows how the satin is caught up into soft folds, held in place by a satin rosette.

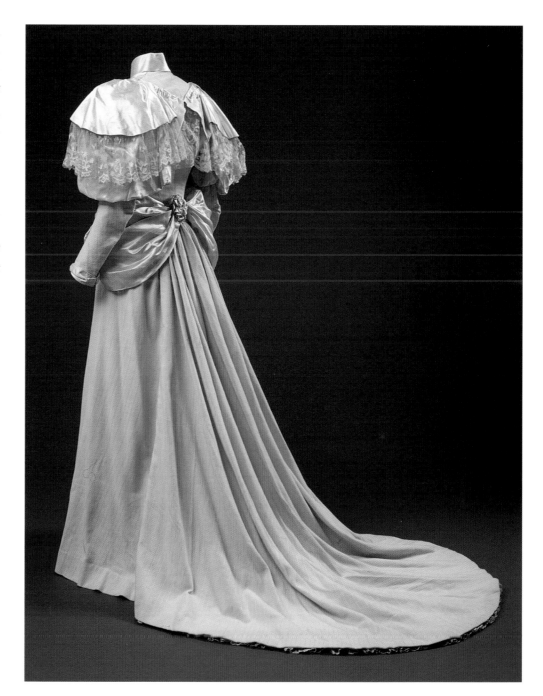

Edwardian Trousseaux

Ladies' underwear, delicately referred to by shopkeepers as 'Ladies' Outfitting' was available in all qualities and materials as ready-made, hand-finished or made-to-measure garments, from the second half of the nineteenth century. By the 1900s, department stores were well established and had become a byword for quality and good service. Much of their hand-worked underwear was the product of convents and charity schools. Theoretically, a city department store could provide the whole wardrobe and trappings for a wedding, from the dress to the iced cake.

In 1898, for those who ordered their trousseau from the Army & Navy Stores, a variety of underclothing and nightwear was available in romantic and picturesque styles, often borrowing elements of dress from the 1820s, in particular the fullness of the sleeves gathered in at the shoulders. The white nightdress with lace insertions and trimmings, dating from the 1890s, was probably part of the trousseau of Pauline Joran, a member of the Carl Rosa Opera Company.

A great variety of corsetry was also at the bride-to-be's disposal. The 1902 Army & Navy catalogue listed estimates from the No.1 trousseau at £10 12s 6d, to No 5 at £52 9s 2d.

The bridal corset shown here was made specially to go under the wedding dress of Grace Palmer, who married James Roach on the Isle of Wight in 1893. It is of silk, formed with flexible whalebone. It has a split metal busk, interlined with kid, fastening at the front, and woven silk laces at the back to draw the corset into an 18-inch (45-cm) waist. A small bow of blue silk is attached to the corset, 'something blue' as in the traditional rhyme

Fashions de Luxe was the catalogue of 1907 for Robinson & Cleaver, 'Linen Manufacturers of Belfast' based in premises in London's Regent Street. The catalogue, only their second publication, took the form of a fashion magazine and the store employed a recognised fashion expert, 'Mrs Aria', who also contributed to *Madame* and the *Lady's Realm*.

DAINTY LINGERIE
AT ROBINSON & CLEAVER, LTD.

Floral Luxury

By the early years of the twentieth century, bouquets for brides and their attendants had reached luxurious proportions. This wedding group was taken at the marriage of Alice Edgeley Watson to Richard Willes on 15 November 1906 in Wayne, Pennsylvania. The bridesmaids are carrying baskets entirely hidden under the flowers and greenery. In our recreation, we have used carnations with leather jacket and asparagus ferns, decorated with broad, structured ribbon.

All the ladies in the photograph are wearing long gloves. Sometimes the bride dispensed with her bouquet, choosing instead to wear a wrist corsage over her gloves. The corsage that we have recreated is made with oriental lilies, with the pollen stamens removed while still in bud, to prevent staining.

The flowers for the wedding breakfast were also becoming very luxurious. Mrs Humphreys in *Manners for Women* observed 'Would it not have appalled our thrifty grandmothers who contented themselves with providing a few vases of flowers for the wedding-breakfast table, and for the beautifying of the drawing room?' She attributes this extravagant fashion, including the 'floral wedding bell' to the influx of heiresses from the New World whose entrance into British society through marriage had been reflected in contemporary literature, such as *The Buccaneers*, written by the American noveliest Edith Wharton and published in 1938, after her death.

Mrs Humphreys noted at a society wedding, 'the wedding bell was composed of the most exquisite exotics, orchids, lilies, roses, gardenias, tuberoses, jessamine, and myrtle, and the hundred or so of tables at which the guests sat had each its lovely burden of snowy blooms enwreathed with smilax'. Another American introduction can be seen in the wedding photograph, groomsmen as well as bridesmaids.

The Wedding Breakfast, Edwardian Style

The 'breakfast' after the wedding ceremony became an established ritual following the change in church regulations in 1886 (p.56). The photograph shows the breakfast table for the marriage on 15 September 1896 in Worksop, Nottinghamshire, of Florence Winks, daughter of a local councillor and butcher, to William Straw, grocer. The bride had married in her travelling dress, of brown and fancy material, with a brown hat to match, and carried a shower bouquet, a gift from her groom. The wedding breakfast was held at the Winks residence: the table dominated by elaborately folded napkins and flower arrangements, including one in a trumpet vase that might have won John Perkins' approval (p.52).

A proposed layout for an early twentieth-century wedding breakfast is again dominated by an exotic plant arrangement, but also by the wedding cake and by bottles of champagne and jellies.

The menu card for a wedding that took place on 27 September 1882 contains the dishes offered that day: Hare soup, Salmon, Roast beef, Turkey, Boiled and Roast fowl, Grouse and partridges, Pigeon pie, Jellied fowl, Lobster, Bridescake, Tipsy cake, Trifle, Vanilla creams, Tartlets, Blancmange, Jellies, Maids of Honour. The dessert included pine(apples), grapes, nectarines, peaches, apples, pears and oranges. This tallies with the menus suggested for wedding breakfasts by Mrs Beeton in her *Book of Household Management*.

The lovely Art Nouveau menu card dates from March 1906, and shows a slightly more restrained list of dishes.

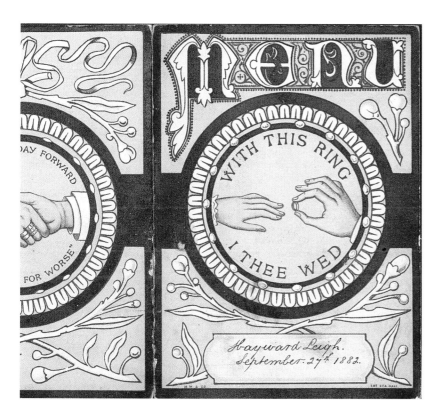

WITH THIS RING I THEE WED

MENU

...DAY FORWARD

...FOR WORSE

Hayward Leigh.
September 27th 1882.

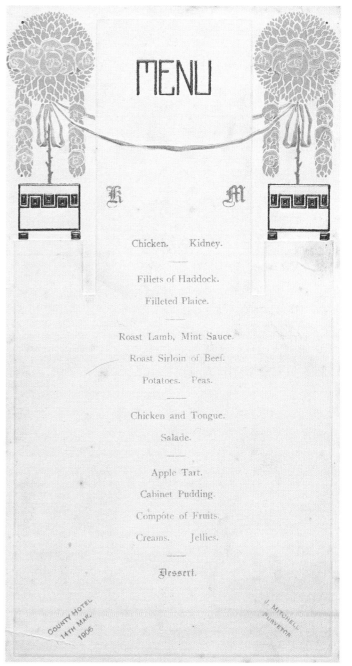

MENU

K   M

Chicken.   Kidney.

Fillets of Haddock.

Filleted Plaice.

Roast Lamb, Mint Sauce.

Roast Sirloin of Beef.

Potatoes.   Peas.

Chicken and Tongue.

Salade.

Apple Tart.

Cabinet Pudding.

Compôte of Fruits.

Creams.   Jellies.

Dessert.

County Hotel
14th May
1906

J. Mitchell
Surveyor

Edwardian Wedding Ephemera

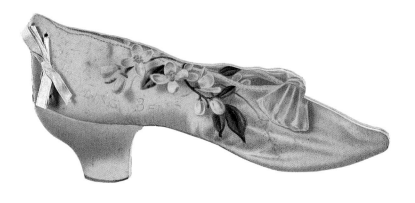

The slipper makes a frequent appearance in wedding customs. At Mary Elizabeth Lucy's wedding in 1823, her bridesmaids threw old satin shoes for luck (p.31). Tradition has it that throwing a slipper after the bride's carriage reflects the transfer of authority from the old home to the new home of her husband. Another tradition was to give the bride's slipper to the groomsmen so that they might drink wine out of it, and toast her long life and happiness. This slipper opens up to provide a poem entitled 'Wedding bells'. It was made by the famous stationery printers, Hildesheimer & Faulkner, who reproduced Beatrix Potter's early illustrations as Christmas cards in the 1890s, thus launching her on her illustrious career. The wedding invitation with its lovely image of the bride holding her bouquet, was also printed by Hildesheimer & Faulkner.

Confetti has enjoyed a long tradition. Originally grain or rice was thrown over the bridal couple as a symbol of fertility. In the eighteenth century, comfits were often thrown, hence *confetti* from the Italian. Another custom had cake broken over the bride's head, a symbol of plenty. Two cakes might be baked, one to break and the other to be iced for the wedding breakfast. In the nineteenth century, paper confetti made its appearance. This advertisement of 1902 marks a further development – scented confetti. It was manufactured by the Patriotic Perfume Company of London and named 'Alexandra' in honour of the new Queen. According to *The Gentleman's Journal* for 1 April 1902, 'being an English-made confetti, it behoves the English public to use it in preference to the foreign confetti which is now on the market, and which is being condemned both by the Press and the medical profession as teeming with almost every known disease'.

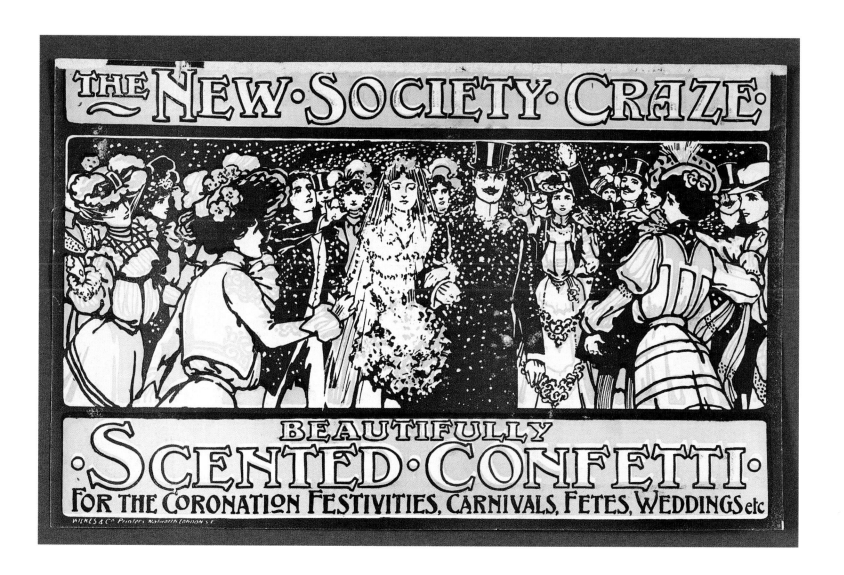

75

Two Edwardian Weddings

The wedding dress on the left dates from 1905, and demonstrates the beauty of the fine wools and laces then available. It is decorated with a skilful combination of handwork, as in the embroidery and the French knots at the waist, and machine work, as in the cutwork and the lace. The low neckline is infilled with lace and a high collar kept rigid by a guimpe boned with celluloid. The dress was made probably for a winter or late spring wedding. We do not know the identity of the bride, but the stylishness of the ensemble, with the silk taffeta underskirt and small train suggests that she came from a middle- or upper middle-class family. The fastening of tiny hooks and eyes would probably have required the services of a lady's maid.

The bridal pair in the photograph are Mr and Mrs F.R.Rowley, who married on 29 June 1909, and are shown in the garden of 22 St David's Hill, Exeter, where the reception was held. Rowley was the curator of the Royal Albert Memorial Museum at the time of the wedding, and his wife took an interest in the museum's dress collection, now kept at Rougemont House in Exeter.

The wedding dress does not survive, but appears to be typical of the period, of ivory or creamy-white satin with a trained skirt. The bodice is constructed slightly higher than the natural waistline, and has soft pleating over the shoulders following current afternoon dress styles. The sleeves seem to have been made from a semi-transparent material, possibly machine lace over chiffon, as was common in dresses of this type. Like the 1905 dress, it has a very high guimpe or stand collar – perhaps the most typically Edwardian aspect of the dress.

The bride's hairstyle is piled high, with a naturalistic head-dress and extremely long tulle veil. She carries a large shower bouquet with enormous June roses and trailing ferns. The groom is formally dressed. His morning suit consists of a smart frock coat with silk facings to the lapels and braid-covered buttons, and pin-stripe trousers. A light-coloured waistcoat, probably white, is worn over a shirt with a turned down collar rather than stiff wings, and a knotted tie instead of a cravat.

Swansong

In 1911, the impresario Serge Diaghilev's company *Les Ballets Russes* took Paris and London by storm. Not only did the dance and music have an enormous impact, but the fashion world was enthralled by the exoticism displayed in the fantastic stage costumes designed by Leon Bakst and others. The French couturier, Paul Poiret, excelled in reproducing this excitement and sense of the cutting edge in his designs. One of his innovations was the hobble skirt which, accompanied by a figure-of-eight garter, restricted the stride of the average healthy woman and caused ridicule and concern. Nevertheless it set the trend for a high-waisted, slim-fitting garment, often cut with a kimono sleeve, a narrow, full-length skirt tapering below the knee and trained, sometimes with a short, full tunic overskirt in a light, contrasting fabric, such as chiffon.

This style was particularly suited to evening dress, but it would seem an unlikely choice for a wedding gown. However, brides liked to be in the vanguard of fashion, and one such wedding dress is in the Killerton collection. It is now very fragile, but can be seen in the wedding photograph (left) of Elfrida Ianthe Clarke and John Gabriel, who married in Paddington in 1914. Elfrida, born in Smyrna in Turkey in 1893, came to London in 1913 as war threatened

Europe. Her dress was made by a fashionable couturier in Smyrna, using diaphanous cream chiffon mounted onto a boned inner bodice of firm cotton, onto which is stitched the waistband of the skirt. The skirt and under bodice are overlaid with a chiffon tunic with a pleated skirt and kimono sleeve cut in one with the bodice. The tunic is trimmed with a deep band of Bruges Duchesse bobbin lace, as well as sprays of orange blossom at the waist and hem.

When war broke out in 1914, brides were encouraged by fashion magazines to dress well to boost morale. The *Girl's Own Annual* devoted a whole page to illustrations of veils for July brides. During the nineteenth century, the veil had usually been pinned to fall over the wreath, but now the reverse was true, the square-shaped veil was placed with the edge of one corner framing the face, the opposite corner falling away to cover the back of the dress. This can be seen in the photograph (left) of the wedding of Mr and Mrs de Smidt in 1914, when the bride borrowed an heirloom lace veil and wore it with circlets of orange blossom.

Mrs de Smidt's dress was purchased from the dressmaker 'Irene', an establishment at 2, The Cathedral Close, then in the heart of what was Exeter's exclusive shopping area. It had a high waistline defined by a broad sash. The sleeves were cut kimono style, in one with the bodice, and fitted tightly to the lower arms ending in a gentle ruffle over the wrists. Typical of the period is the combination of extremely rich and heavy fabrics, here represented by the brocade, and lightweight delicate materials such as fine jap-silk and chiffon. The lace edging along the waist has been carefully wired to make it stand out, adding to the exotic appearance.

Married in Khaki

The early, carefree attitude towards bridal fashion (see previous pages) did not last long. As the conditions in Flanders grew ever more horrific, so weddings became plainer. Frivolity was felt to be inappropriate and weddings were brought forward as men were called up. The photograph of a wedding in 1917 shown here is typical. The groom, a sergeant in the medical corps, is in uniform, his bride wears a calf-length, loose-fitting tiered lace gown. The fringed silk sash, almost casually tied, lends a slight air of exoticism to the ensemble. Her veil appears to be of plain tulle with a band of blossom fixed to one side.

A correspondent to *Housewife* magazine in 1941 recalled the difficulty in obtaining materials during the First World War: 'We industriously ornamented our frocks with hand embroidery when wool and silk *galons*, *passementerie* and braids disappeared from the luxury list... . Buttons, beloved by the dozen on their frocks by the Edwardians and Victorians, being made of paper were inclined to dissolve in a shower of rain, and take upon themselves the shape of convulvulus when their day's work is done. So, we made our frocks to slip on over the head without buttons.'

Family tradition has it that the very chic, two-piece tailored costume was worn for a Dublin wedding in 1915. The bridegroom, an Irish clergyman, had been called up for a foreign posting as an army chaplain, so the wedding was arranged at short notice. The outfit consists of a fine navy serge coat and skirt fastened onto a silk blouse with a mock waistcoat front. The jacket lapels are faced with satin, and the front trimmed with buttons which conceal the real fastenings, hooks and eyes, stitched beneath. The coat has a short peplum and a buckled half-belt at the back. The long sleeves have turned-back cuffs. The skirt is narrow for the year – in general, skirts had become fuller and shorter by 1915 – but this dress still has a long panelled skirt with a 'hobble' band towards the hem, finished with a button. The smartness of the tailored suit is set off by the thin silk blouse. The waistcoat front is carried out in striped moire silk with three chestnut-shaped metal-cased pearl buttons showing above and below the coat fastening. The broad lapels were intended to be worn over the neckline of the coat, adding to the stylish look.

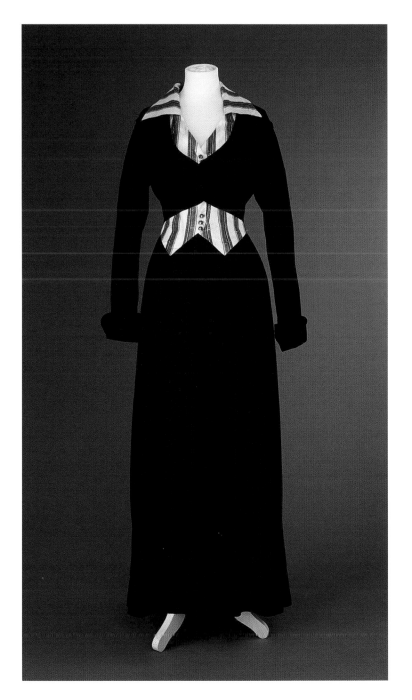

War and Peace

Oriental styles continued to influence couture right through to the end of the First World War. The cream Chinese silk dress with a vermicular pattern (right) was worn by an unknown bride *c*. 1917-8. The collar and sleeves are daintily finished with chiffon, pleated into a tiny fan at the cuff, and embellished with small glass beads. The high necked bodice looks back to the years preceding the war, but the natural waistline and 'barrel-line' skirt, full at the hips, date the dress.

Much more utilitarian, although still elegant, is a fine cream wool suit that is said to have been worn at a wedding in 1919 (opposite above and detail below). The long tailored coat and full skirt are trimmed with a wide silk braid: the decorative painted metal buttons add a glint of gold to the ensemble.

Frivolity returned with the new decade or, as *Vogue* put it, 'fashion has supplanted custom and individuality has supplanted both'. Hemlines rose and fell, but the garçonne line remained essentially the same – loose and low-waisted, minimising the bust. Popular materials were lace laid over white or coloured satin, crepe de chine, silk taffeta, tulle, chiffon and lamé or silver tissue, with velvet the favourite for winter months.

The bride who married on 1 September 1920 at East Budleigh in Devon chose a romantic yet modern short-sleeved, calf-length dress with tulle 'panniers' attached to the hips and falling into handkerchief points at the side of the embroidered net overdress (opposite right).

The skirt is composed of net machine embroidered in a large floral repeat in white and silver, and the bodice of tulle. The dress is lined with cream silk, and has its own under-bodice, lined with cotton and boned to support the gentle folds of fine tulle.

Two Royal Weddings

Two royal weddings that took place in the early 1920s were widely reported. When the Princess Royal, daughter of King George V and Queen Mary, married Henry, Viscount Lascelles in 1922, she wore a dress of traditional silver, with a court train decorated with floral emblems and an overdress embroidered with pearls and beads. The veil was an old family piece of heavy Honiton lace. She is shown with her parents and her bridegroom in the photograph on the left.

More innovative was the dress worn by Lady Elizabeth Bowes-Lyon when she married Albert, Duke of York, second son of the King and Queen, in 1923 (right). Her dress was inspired by medieval Italy and as such set a trend for brides to copy. The ivory chiffon moire was decorated with one vertical and three horizontal bands of silver lamé, and further ornamented with seed pearls. She wore two trains, suspended from the shoulder and the waistline. The dress was designed by Madame Handley Seymour.

In an article entitled 'The Bridal Toilette and some Beautiful Creations in the Royal Trousseau', *Country Life* dived into enthusiastic detail: 'Words are poor, inadequate things wherewith to describe the slight, slim figure as she walked up the aisle in her long, full though clinging gown of tenderest ivory moire, the full overskirt, with its short train, falling apart in front over a petticoat that literally touched the ground ...'.

Queen Mary lent her future daughter-in-law her Flanders lace veil. Many of the society ladies attending the wedding also wore lace, and the gathering was seen as a boost to the Nottingham-based industry. *Country Life* continues: 'Over a fond of net bordered with ... Nottingham lace, and broad line of silver galon down the centre the veil of royal dentelle fell from the head, where it was held by a delicate chaplet of green leaves that finished either side with a posy of small white roses and white heather.'

A Suffolk Bride

A recent acquisition of the Killerton collection is a ready-made wedding dress of 1925. The bride, twenty-two-year-old Elsie Grimsey, married Edward Daldry, four years her senior. Edward, one of thirteen children, was a herdsman, while Elsie had worked in her family's market garden. After the wedding, the dress, petticoat, veil and wreath were tenderly put away in their original packaging and were only rediscovered after Elsie's death in 1974.

The dress is made of extremely fine cream silk, with chiffon collar and cuffs edged with a dainty cotton machine lace. A row of diamanté 'buttons' and a mock belt trim the front of the dress, which follows contemporary day dress styles and has a fashionably low waistline. The silk is so fine as to be transparent, and was worn over a knitted silk slip.

The veil is typical of the period, of a square, open mesh net with a border of machine-tamboured silk and corner floral motif. The wedding photograph shows the bride wearing her head-dress and veil low over her brow in the fashion of the 1920s. A variety of head-dresses were worn at this time, from the simplest bandeau of silver or satin thread fastened with knots of artificial flowers at the side of the head, to tiaras and diadems of paste, diamanté or wired lace. However, traditions die hard, and wax buds of orange blossom, myrtle and pearls were prevalent. Elsie has chosen a wax tiara with star-like blossoms.

The one item of dress not included in the bride's box are her shoes. The wedding photograph shows that she wore satin shoes with bar-straps. We have substituted a pair of bar shoes decorated with beading that were made for a grander wedding.

Frequently veils and head-dresses survive separately from the dress. In spite of their obvious fragility, the commonest way of fulfilling the need to wear 'something old' was achieved through the loan of a veil, or veil and head-dress. The Killerton collection has several examples dating from the 1920s and '30s, preserved because they were worn by the brides' daughters during the 1940s and '50s.

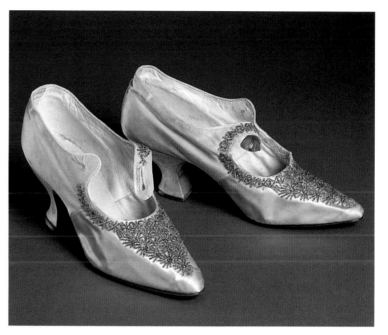

Petals and Tassels

Hems of dresses in the 1920s were often scalloped or ended in handkerchief points. Deeply petalled dresses are worn by the adult bridesmaids in a London wedding group from the mid-1920s. The little bridesmaid wears a wired cap to look like a Dutch head-dress. The Killerton collection has two such hats, created from machine lace over a wire form.

Mabs Fashions for March 1925 advocated a daffodil and tulip bride,
declaring 'the white bride is no longer <u>the</u> thing'. The model is wearing a frock of yellow georgette with pearl trimming and tassels. Her veil of ivory lace is held in place by tinted yellow orange blossoms, and she carries a bouquet of yellow tulips. The spring flower theme continues with a crocus bridesmaid, in shaded mauve georgette. The matching tulle veil is held in position at the ears by a clump of flowers and tinsel ribbon band. Her round, tight bouquet is reminiscent of

those fashionable for mid-nineteenth-century weddings.

The superb dress dates from 1929, with the latest fashionable shape and a scalloped hemline. The flared skirt is lower at the back, and the waistline has a low point at the centre of the front, a slightly medieval influence. The decoration on the fine silk slipper satin is extremely elaborate. A chiffon panel at the centre front of the skirt is weighted with pearl, silver thread and bead embroidery. Crystal beading and silver thread embroidery produce a *trompe l'oeil* bow effect on the bodice below the rounded neckline. It is not known who made the dress, but it is most likely that it was made to measure by a skilled court dressmaker. The veil also survives, of full-length tulle with an attached head-dress of pearls and orange blossom.

Young Attendants

It was fashionable at this period to have an entourage of very young bridesmaids, often picturesquely dressed. Celia and Katharine Jones were four and a half years old when they wore high yoked satin dresses and simple gathered mob caps (above right). They were the twin daughters of the Rector of Shepton Mallet in Somerset, who performed the marriage ceremony for Dolly Wainwright and Kenneth Durrant in 1919. After the wedding, the dresses were altered for best wear (below right).

During the First World War and in the 1920s, shorter dresses in silk, tulle, organdie or muslin were popular for bridesmaids, although full-length gowns still made an appearance depending on the taste of the bride. Fashion still favoured white or sugary pastel colours: three examples can be seen on the far right. The full-length, high yoked dress dates from *c*. 1920. The pretty rosebud printed tulle is overlaid on a silk dress. The high waistline would have been marked by a sash, probably pink, and the yoke is covered by a frilled chiffon fichu in Kate Greenaway style (pp.64-5).

The blue silk taffeta dress is an example of a shorter style worn by a grown-up bridesmaid. The dress has a plain, sleeveless bodice and dropped waistline, with a petal skirt elaborately appliquéd with organdie hand embroidered in white, and with silk and metal thread rosebuds.

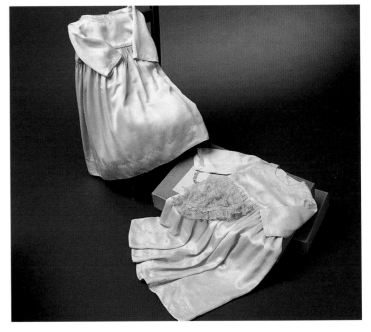

The plain peach-coloured dress is for a child. With its short, gathered sleeves it probably dates from the mid-1930s, and is full length, echoing glamorous adult styles. All-over machine lace became fashionable again at this time. Lace day dresses with flared skirts and butterfly sleeves were an option for summer weddings.

Groomsmen as well as adult bridesmaids are known to have formed part of bridal processions from the sixteenth century. Victorian page-boys were rigged out in formal fancy dress and often acted as train-bearers. One wedding in 1885 had little boys dressed in dark blue plush suits lined with gold satin and lace collars in the style of Little Lord Fauntleroy, as immortalised by Frances Hodgson Burnett. The late Victorian photograph below shows a five-year-old dressed in eighteenth-century court costume with his 'Kate Greenaway' companion. Highland dress was a perennial favourite: page-boys in tartan kilt can be seen in the nineteenth century on p.41 and in the twentieth on p.119.

A North Country Bride

Flower, Lady Furness, of Bedburn Hall, Co. Durham, was married in 1929 and presented at court the following year. Her dress is a good example of how wedding gowns could be modified for the first presentation as a married woman. It is made of exquisite silk satin in a pale, pinkish shade of cream, cut with a flared skirt, with slightly more length at the back. Originally it had full-length sleeves that were removed for the court presentation. The train is of old lace, lined with chiffon, and the simple dress is finished with a pearl girdle. The underwear was also kept. A simple cream silk bandeau bra and knickers timmed with Honiton lace and hand embroidered with a lucky horseshoe in blue and white – a note of 'something blue', as usual, concealed.

Amongst the accessories is the original wedding veil and wreath of lovely and unusual design, with a handwritten reminder from the supplier, 'B.H.S.R.': 'Parchment net veil and orange blossom wreath – Kindly draw up the head piece of the veil by the ribbon tying it up at the back. The short point goes to the front and the long one to the back. The wreath is the exact measurement of your hats so I hope it will be all right. The bunches at the sides can be pinched up a little more if necessary to make them smaller.'

The photograph shows Lady Furness descending from the limousine, with the flower wreath duly in place, and her spectacular shower bouquet.

The Economics of the Bottom Drawer

Brides had to work hard to furnish their 'bottom drawer'. When Maud Galen married Leonard Buckeridge in 1929, she kept detailed accounts of every penny spent on her wedding dress and trousseau. A diary containing a list of wedding gifts and thirty-three receipts are preserved with her wedding outfit at Killerton. The veil is the only article not to survive.

The dress is simply cut with a skirt reaching to just over the knee, and full-length sleeves. The material is a rich cream, silk brocade with a large leaf pattern, suggesting an early date, perhaps as early as 1890, although family tradition states that Maud's gown was taken from material left over from a dress made for a relative's silver wedding celebrations in 1911.

Maud did not go out to work, but helped her mother at home, managing a family of thirteen. From ten shillings a week, she managed to provide her trousseau. Her calculations show that the wedding dress and shoes cost a total of £4. The material was provided, so the dressmaker, Madame Hyde of Peckham, in South London, had only to be paid for the making up: she charged £1 15s 6d. However, the costliest item was the going-away outfit, at £5.

The total cost of Maud's trousseau was £30 (the modern equivalent would be £553). She listed each item as follows:

Wedding dress and shoes	£4
Going away and fur collar	£5
2 pair shoes	£4
Undies	£2
Corsets	£2
Stockings	£2
Hats	£2
Mat.[material] for dresses	£2
Spring coat	£4
Sundries	£2
Total	£30

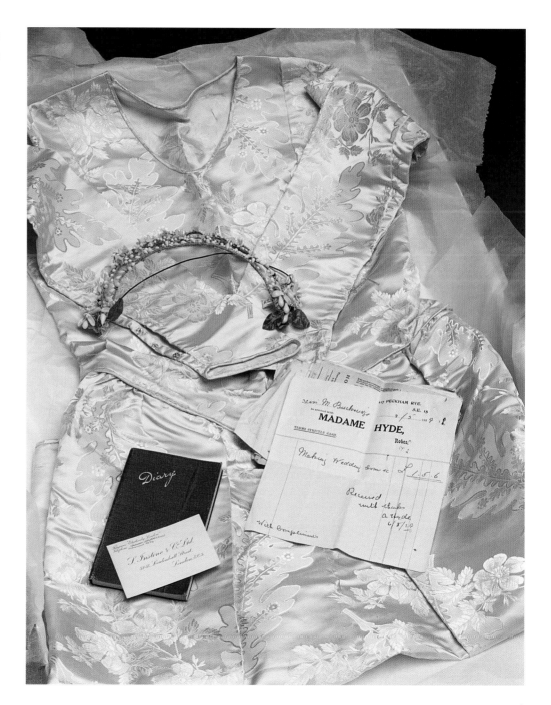

Trousseaux, 1920s and '30s

e wide skirt so much | across and across yo
the
ar-
o.
ed
ur
ve
on
for
an
If
ce-
i-
ge
ur
ed
el-
rie
e,
is
ne-
in-

in
ng
ur
rm
es
m-
ur
as
an
ey
er.
ver
d
op
rt,
in
he
ns.
he
en
ice
ur
ost
to

No. 50,266.
(34-40in. bust.)

TO GET YOUR CUT-

al order and coupon! In medium weight

yo
sti
fro
wi
ov
yo

th
pe
bli
on
eff
de
c c
ma
sic
sti
en
fro
yo
lo
lit
an
sa
in
ru

up
en
yo
or
tra

6y
are
wi
a
fu
wl
bii
str
lin
1/in
4

Underwear became less bulky and more complicated in the years between the two world wars. With the increasing availability of man-made fibres, a wide range of materials was used, with manufacturers giving their products distinctive and often glamorous names. Artificial silk (rayon) was very popular in both woven and knitted forms, selling under various trade names. An advertisement for 'Tarantulle' made by the Manchester firm, Tootals, emphasised the non-fading qualities of this fabric: 'Have you seen Betty's trousseau? She has the loveliest things. All hand-made and such becoming colours.'

Those with a limited dress allowance would buy lingerie made up at a charitable institution or make them at home. Women's magazines often gave away patterns or offered a mail order service. The 'cut-out' advertised in the *Woman's Friend* of 20 February 1926 was a pair of camiknickers (left). 'It is almost impossible to imagine anything more fascinating than the lingerie of today' states the copy accompanying the instructions for making up this garment.

Combination garments in fine materials soon left behind their old image of unattractive utilitarian garments. They allowed a paring down of the silhouette to suit first the garçonne line of the 1920s, with a low waist, short skirts to the knee and a minimised bust, and in the 1930s the slim figure achieved through diet and exercise. 'The slightest lump will betray itself; if you eat a grape, it will show; the one piece garment is the only solution' warned *Vogue* in 1932.

The 'Charming Lingerie' pictured here comes from *Roma's Pictorial Fashions*. They were intended to be made up in 'Crêpe Caliste' manufactured by Ferguson Brothers and available in pastel shades.

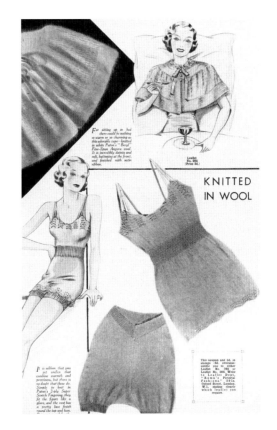

KNITTED IN WOOL

The other page from the same magazine shows both wool and silk underwear, including 'exquisite camiknickers' by Daphne, a famous lingerie shop in London's South Molton Street. Less appealing at first glance are the knitted wool vest and knickers – one suspects that the fashion drawing adds a much more glamorous aspect than they deserve. Nevertheless, such garments had a place in a bride's trousseau: Maud Buckeridge listed a sensible 'vest' in her accounts (p.94).

CHARMING LINGERIE— —designed for Roma's Own Material!

Sylphs and Madonnas

Bridal gowns of the mid-1930s were influenced by the glamorous evening dresses worn by Hollywood filmstars, and by the dress worn by Princess Marina of Greece at her wedding in 1934 to the Duke of Kent, fourth son of King George V and Queen Mary (above). The Princess's dress was designed by the fashionable French couturier, Edward Molyneux, and took the form of a sheath, cut on the cross, with wide hanging sleeves, giving it a medieval look. It was made up in a specially woven white and silver brocade, recalling the traditional combination for royal brides.

The dress was widely copied in all its details, perhaps because of its simplicity. Nevertheless this simplicity could be misleading, for such dresses were a triumph of skilled cutting and fitting.

When Dorothy P. Alma Martin married Noblett Carter, a guardsman of the Royal Artillery, at St Mary's Church, Dartington in Devon on 4 September 1934, she wore just such a dress, probably designed by Worth. Of fine silk satin, it has a draped cowl neckline, curved train and medieval-style sleeves. The style is echoed in the outfits of her bridesmaids, who wear tulle Juliet caps edged with silver leaves. Her veil of Limerick lace was a family heirloom, worn with a turquoise blue headband, recalling the tradition of 'something blue'. This is one of a series of photographs of the smart society wedding – they all feature the bride's pet spaniel, Sam, adorned with a satin bow and leash.

The bride dispensed with flowers, carrying instead a handbag of cream satin made from her aunt's Edwardian wedding dress. Her bridesmaids are shown carrying large bouquets of roses, but the flower favoured at this period was the Madonna lily, reinforcing the medieval look. We have recreated a bouquet of lilies in the characteristic 'shower' style. The head-dress by Hesta Singlewood also uses the lily shape.

The Practical Bride

A practical bride chose a wedding dress that could be worn for many occasions. The *Essex County Standard* noted in 1931 'after you take off your veil, you slip into a little bolero jacket with elbow sleeves banded in white fox or ermine which will make a perfect evening ensemble'.

The dress in printed, flowered georgette in shades of blue, pink

and yellow made an appropriate wedding gown for a summer's day. Such dresses were versatile, and could be adapted for other occasions long after the wedding celebrations were over. This dress is made with a bloused bodice and clinging skirt,

flaring out towards the hem, finished with two frills of georgette. The matching coatee has short ruched sleeves and turn back lapels. It was worn at the wedding of Hilda Burrow to Walter Darch in 1937.

The couple in the photograph above

were married on 31 August 1933. The bride wears summery printed chiffon with a rayon lining. Rayon is not necessarily easy to maintain, and while ironing the dress the night before the wedding, the bride scorched and melted the fabric. She patched the spoilt piece with pink paper and no one was the wiser. The dress was worn with a matching coatee and wide brimmed summer hat in crin braid. Her husband wore a smart suit, turned-down collar and tie, with a trilby hat.

'By 1930 the wedding dress had been taken out of the fashion scene proper', so declared the fashion writer Prudence Glynn in *Fashion and Dress in the Twentieth Century*. The 'groom' shown in the photograph on the further left is wearing the standard morning suit with grey trousers and tail-coat that has become fossilised as traditional formal wedding clothing for men. His dapper suit is completed by a silk top hat and grey gloves. This fashion shot by Greville of Watford was probably taken as an advertisement for an outfitter. His model companion poses in full bridal dress, probably of white silk or rayon satin, with a long beaded train in silver lamé. The tulle veil, held on by a narrow circlet of artificial buds, is charmingly ruched around the face, rather than set low down on the crown.

High Sheen Satins

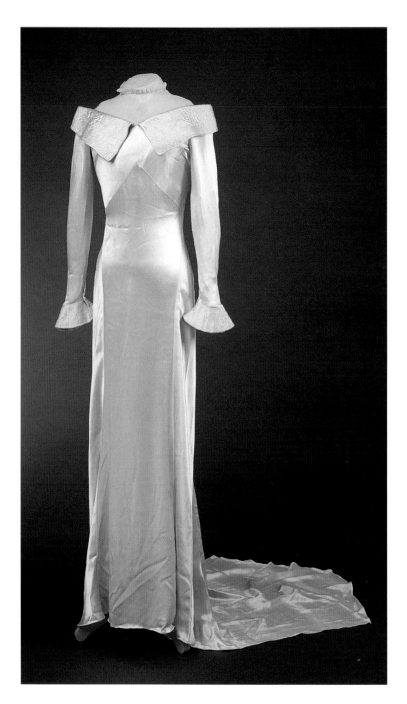

The wedding dress shown on the left dates from 1935. It is extremely tight-fitting, made for a very slender bride. The favoured materials at this time were fluid and slippery, with a high sheen, such as satins in silk and rayon. These could be made up in ivory, cream, pinkish-white, and a pale blue-white tone. A pink wedding dress of the 1930s with its silver girdle is shown flat together with the cold white satin dress described below.

With the end of the 1930s came a new mood. The film *Gone with the Wind*, featuring the lavish ballgowns of the 1860s, was released in 1939, but nineteenth-century dress was already influencing fashion. The upper silhouette was emphasised with

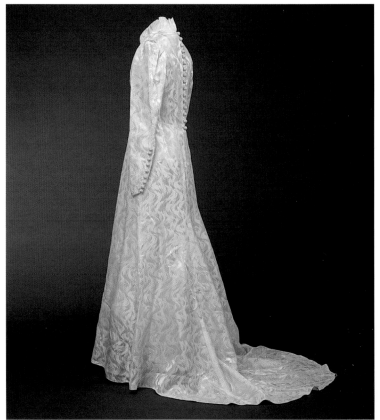

high necklines, stand-up collars, and padded shoulders. At its most extreme, the Victorian revival included full skirts over crinolines, sometimes with panniers and bustles to emphasise the hips and back.

When Rose Johnson married Vic Reynolds at Willenhall in Staffordshire on 13 July 1940, she eschewed the crinoline look, but chose a very elegant dress with stand-up collar and a long train extending from the centre back. The sleeves are gathered over the shoulders, narrowing to fit tightly to the arm with nine covered buttons. The back of the dress fastens with sixteen covered buttons, providing plenty of work for the bridesmaid and the bride's mother when dressing the bride on her wedding day.

Ingenuity and Improvisation

Measures introduced in the early part of the Second World War had a profound effect upon what was possible for brides to wear at their weddings. In October 1940 purchase tax was introduced, driving up the price of textiles. Clothes rationing was first announced on 1 June 1941, allowing 66 coupons per person annually. These could be used for dress materials and knitting wool as well as made-up clothing. The Board of Trade promoted a 'Make Do and Mend' campaign, issuing advice on prolonging the life of clothes and instructions on recycling old garments. A utility scheme was also introduced, with strict regulations prohibiting, for instance, the number of pleats in a skirt and the amount of material to be used. Utility clothing was recognisable from the CC41 label.

Against this background, those determined to have a white wedding improvised. One way was to use cheaper synthetic materials. The department store, Derry & Toms, for instance, in 1944 advertised a rayon satin dress for £13 15s 6d and seven clothing coupons. A year earlier, Eileen Holland wore a plain, unpatterned dress of rayon silk (right) for her wedding on 19 July. With its padded and quilted yoke and hem, it has the look of a nightdress. The bride wore an antique lace veil with a circlet of orange blossom in the traditional style.

Other brides borrowed their wedding dresses, or used those worn by their mothers. When Joyce Rogers married Captain J.G.Wood RM at Broadclyst church on the Killerton estate on 19 April 1945, she wore the dress in which her mother had been married in Trinidad in 1908. Of very fine, lightweight cream silk, the dress was suitable for a warmer climate than that of Devon. Although it was not altered for Joyce's wedding, it would have been worn over a corset and suitably shaped petticoat the first time round – hence the rather droopy effect in the 1945 photograph.

Leave Permitting

In peacetime, weddings could be planned for months ahead, and the dress, trousseau and flowers carefully chosen. Wartime weddings were often arranged on the spur of the moment, when the long-awaited telegram announcing the bridegroom's arrival on forty-eight-hour leave spurred a rush to obtain a licence.

Molly Craven was working as a VAD nurse at a military hospital near Macclesfield when she met her husband-to-be, Sub-Lieutenant John Casson. A date was chosen for the wedding, 20 March 1943, but as John was due to return to command a supply boat, he left Molly to make the wedding arrangements. Molly hitch-hiked to Blackpool to have fittings for her dress, made by Madame Skelton, a high-class dressmaker. But John's boat was engaged in battle with a German ship and he was taken prisoner. For more than two years Molly and John kept in touch by letter, until John arrived home on 16 May 1945. Ten days later the couple were married at Siddington Church near Alderley Edge in Cheshire, and Molly was at last able to wear her elegant wedding dress (far right). It is very cleverly cut, of white wool crepe fitted tightly to the figure, and a square train. The dress is trimmed with broad bands of cream velvet at the bodice and hem.

The other dress in the photograph was

worn by Patience Dunstan when she married Dr F.F.Cartwright on a foggy day, 20 December 1941, at Trottiscliffe near Maidstone in Kent. Mrs Cartwright recalled 'very few people wore white unless they were lent a pre-war dress. Mine ... was too long, so Jay's made the hat from the un-needed hem and embroidered it to match the belt'. Jay's of Regent Street in London were a long-established firm that had run a court dressmaking service since the nineteenth century. The dress is a fashionable full-length style in blue-grey rayon crêpe, with a matching belt and hat trimmed with applied gold braid and embroidery.

The accessories included a pair of blue and grey fabric sandals with wedge heels. Leather was in short supply, so wartime shoes were manufactured with cork or wooden heels, often wedge-shaped and chunky in appearance. As 'something old', Patience wore a pair of nineteenth-century machine knitted lace mittens which are preserved with the dress. Her bouquet, of cream roses, freesias and gardenias, came from Constance Spry, the famous florist who was a friend of her uncle: 'This is perhaps why the flower were un-wartime like, especially for December. I can still remember the wonderful smell.'

Demobilisation

War may have been over by 1945, but austerity continued. Clothes were rationed until the early 1950s, and many items were manufactured for export only. It was still common for brides to marry in their best, rather than a one-off white gown. The bridal couple shown in front of the church porch were married in Maisemore, Gloucestershire on 4 June 1945, the day before the Allies assumed full control throughout Germany. The groom is wearing a 'de-mob' suit, his bride a smart ensemble with dark hat and gloves, and a floral corsage instead of a bouquet.

The second bridal pair are Mr and Mrs Green, who married in Devon on 18 June 1949. She is wearing a day dress of grey crêpe with grey fern leaf embroidery. The accessories are a grey felt Connor hat trimmed with pink artificial flowers, and a bouquet of flowers chosen to match the hat trim. The hat is in keeping with the 'New Look' style, launched in 1947 by Christian Dior, and highly fashionable in the late 1940s.

Underneath the dress, the bride wore a lace-trimmed cream silk slip and knickers made of parachute silk. Included in her trousseau was a pair of ruched pink nylon camiknickers, the first nylon underwear she had been able to purchase. At the time nylon, developed by DuPont and

launched in 1938, was still scarce and its novelty made it desirable.

The pink nylon camiknickers, together with cream lace bra and pants, show the return to glamour at last for British women. The bra and knickers, imports from China, are pre-war.

Trousseaux, 1940s and '50s

LOVELY UNDERWEAR does something to a girl—gives her a feeling of *film star* extravagance. And any girl can indulge her extravagant fancies without being a spend-thrift if she makes her own underwear with Ferguson Lingerie Fabrics. Fergoneen—designed for luxury, irresistible colours and patterns costs only 2/11½ a yard. Crepe Juliesyl, a heavier weight fabric—patterned costs 2/11½ or plain costs 1/11½ a yard. Carlisette—filmy fine in plain colours costs only 1/11½ a yard.

Ask your draper to show you the latest ranges.

'I'm NOT extravagant – I made it myself with Fergoneen' announces the wearer of the camiknickers in an advertisement c.1940. Rayon yarns woven into a variety of fabrics from heavy dress crêpes to fine, lightweight lingerie fabrics were widely used during the 1940s. They were often printed in appropriate patterns and colours, usually pastel shades for lingerie. Ready-to-wear underwear was more often than not sold in ubiquitous shades of peach, pale green and white.

Weldon's home dressmaking magazine was a long established publication. Issue no.718, 'Undies', offered more than sixty designs for underwear and nightwear in the 1950s. A variety of camiknickers, french knickers, slips and full-skirted half slips are shown here. The very full waist petticoat on a slim hip yoke was designed to give 'swing to your full skirted frocks'.

The designs are pretty, light and feminine, with lace frills and flounces, scalloped hems and ribbons. From 1947, when Christian Dior launched his 'New Look', short boxy styles were left behind, and many women adopted these full-skirted clothes. Evening dress especially was heavily influenced by the crinoline era of the nineteenth century, with suitable underwear to support the line. Once again, the emphasis was on a tiny waist. Corsets returned in the form of waspies, corselettes and long line brassières in boned elasticated lace and nylon fabrics. Nylon, developed by DuPont in the late 1930s and launched in 1938, was now more readily available. The undergarments pictured here might just as easily be made up in nylon as the old rayon 'artificial silk' and natural silks and cottons. Cotton and nylon machine laces and rayon ribbons could also be purchased inexpensively from a local haberdashery.

Trousseau Charm

Weldons Pattern No. 8473 Camiknickers in pretty lingerie print. For 36 inch bust: 1⅝ yards 36 inch material, no one way. Price by post, 2s. **No. 1565** Slim-waisted Slip. For 36 inch bust: 2⅜ yards 36 inch plain material; 1½ yards lace. Price by post. 2s. 3d. **No. 3005** Lace and ribbon-trimmed Camisole and Petticoat. For 36 inch bust: 2⅜ yards 36 inch material. Price by post, 2s. 3d. **No. 5253** Lovely Nightie. For 36 inch bust: 3⅜ yards 36 inch material; ½ yard 4 inch insertion. Price by post, 2s. **No. 7423** Scalloped Pyjamas. For 36 inch bust: 4⅜ yards 36 inch material, no one way. Price by post, 2s. **No. 1405** Evening Petticoat, in ballet length. For 40 inch hips: 4⅜ yards 36 inch plain material. Price by post, 2s. 3d. **No. 1545** Demure Nightie. For 36 inch bust: 3⅞ yards 36 inch material, no one way. Price by post, 2s. 3d.

Weldons Pattern No. 3823 Gay young Housecoat, buttoning right up the front. For 36 inch bust: 5¼ yards (or long sleeves, 6 yards) 36 inch material, no one way; ½ yard contrast. Price by post, 2s. **No. 1655** Very full Waist Petticoat on a slim hipyoke. Give swing to your full skirted frocks! For 40 inch hips: 2½ yards 36 inch plain material. Price by post, 2s. 3d. **No. 2203** French Knickers and Panties. For 40 inch hips: knickers 1½ yards, panties 1 yard 36 inch plain material. Price by post, 2s. **No. 2195** Frill-edged Petticoat and Briefs to match, very easy to make. For 40 inch hips: 3 yards 36 inch material. Price by post, 2s. 3d. **No. 2545** is a charming Slip and Knicker set. Note the lace-elastic band at waist of knickers. For 36 inch bust: 3½ yards 36 inch plain material; 5½ yards 2 inch lace. Price by post, 2s. 3d.

WELDONS PATTERNS on these two pages : Nos. 1405, 1655, 2203 and 2195 in hip sizes 36 to 44; others in bust sizes 32 to 40.

Business as Usual

Although the Second World War ended in 1945, austerity and frugality continued to dominate many people's lives. Brides in the 1950s often chose not to have one-off white gowns, but to wear dresses that could be used afterwards for special occasions. The

pale blue silk dress shown here was purchased ready-made in Nairobi, Kenya, for a wedding in the late 1950s. The dress is in a fashionable day style, with short full skirt, and round, high neckline. It fastens at the back with a row of large covered buttons and a bow. Dresses of this type were held out with their own integral underskirts, or the addition of a stiff nylon net petticoat.

The pale green dress dates from 1960. Of heavy rayon satin, it is embellished with ornate bead embroidery on the skirt, as can be seen in the details. The bride-to-be saw it in a shop window and fell in love with it, although it was originally designed by Frank Usher as a cocktail dress. The dress shop, Frances Dee of Romford in Essex, added sleeves to make it more appropriate for the wedding, which took place at Caxton Hall in London in March 1960. The bride wore a small 'Juliet' cap with pink feathers and pink satin shoes, specially dyed to pick up the beading on the dress.

The huge bouquets carried by brides and their attendants throughout the first half of the twentieth century gave way to much more modest arrangements from 1940 onwards. This bridesmaid at a wedding in September 1955 is carrying a small bouquet of yellow flowers to match her yellow taffeta dress, overlaid with yellow spotted net.

The recreation shows a similar bouquet for bride or bridesmaid, with roses in ivory and yellow, freesias, and leather leaf and asparagus fern. Not only were bouquets much smaller, but with a defined shape. Strongly influenced by Constance Spry, the most popular bridal flowers of the 1950s and '60s were lily of the valley, stephanotis, gardenias, camellias and bud hyacinth.

Also in the photograph is the short veil worn by Angela Aggett when she married Barry Kerslake on 5 September 1959 at Whipton in Exeter. It is of fine embroidered net with a coronet of tiny seed pearls and waxed orange blossom. The crystal necklace was a gift from her groom.

The Return of Glamour

When Princess Elizabeth, elder daughter of King George VI and Queen Elizabeth, married her cousin Prince Philip Mountbatten on 20 November 1947, she wore a dress that combined glamour and prettiness to signal the end of grim years of war – though rationing continued into the 1950s. According to the designer, Norman Hartnell, 10,000 pearls were imported from America for the dress. It was made in embroidered silk satin from the Scottish firm, Winthertur, near Dunfermline, while the square-shaped train, fifteen yards in length, was woven at Lullingstone in Kent. Hartnell gave the dress a sweetheart neckline, then very much in vogue. The tulle veil cascaded from a diamond fringe tiara.

Highly publicised celebrity weddings attracted as much attention as royal occasions. The two were combined in the marriage of the film actress Grace Kelly to Prince Rainier of Monaco in 1956. The bride wore an exquisite Brussels lace dress that inspired many imitations, although few could aspire to the luxury of costly 'real' lace.

The very elegant pure white silk dress shown here was a model gown by Bianchi, made for Cleo Whitten for her first marriage to Peter Andrew Tomei in Boston, USA on 30 May 1959. The dress is every bride's dream. Cut with a fairly

high waist and short plain sleeves, it is reminiscent of an eighteenth-century sackback gown, with fullness at the hips and a long train pleated into the back of the dress and marked by a bow. Cleo wore an embroidered veil over her fashionably short hair cut in an 'urchin' style. Her sister acted as maid of honour: she is shown in the photograph wearing a cocktail-length version of the bridal gown with high-heeled satin shoes and a sheer crin hat with wide brim.

The End is the Beginning

During the 1960s, dress and accessories varied between the very modern and romantic, nostalgic themes, calling upon a combination of influences from 'peasant' to historical dress. This interest in historical dress has continued to the present day. Recent revivals have included the corset bodice derived from eighteenth-century styles, introduced by Vivienne Westwood in her collections during the 1980s and '90s and now established as a standard aspect of bridal wear. Another is the fashion for Regency style dresses inspired by film productions of Jane Austen novels. Hesta Singlewood's designs for head-dresses also reflect the historical interest. Her feather head-dress shown opposite above is reminiscent of the plain, classical half-hat style of the late 1950s, early '60s.

The bride in the photographs is Julia Thomas, who married

Terence Harris on 15 August 1964 at Gerrard's Cross in Buckinghamshire. The bride's mother purchased the dress ready-made at a local boutique. It is in the slim and narrow fitting 'empire line' style of the late eighteenth and early nineteenth centuries, a cut that had already enjoyed two revivals

during the 1890s and from c. 1909. The material is ivory rayon satin with a jacquard pattern, featuring a design of sprays of lily of the valley and fern. The train was made separately and attached to the waist seam at the back of the dress. The veil is typical of the late 1950s and early 1960s, short and made up of three layers of tulle stitched onto a plastic comb. Two large decorative organdie flowers are also fixed onto the comb.

The other wedding dress shown here is quite different in style, though the white satin and lace with metallic threads recalls the richness of eighteenth-century bridal clothes. Sheila Ashby purchased the fabrics for the dress and coat in Glasgow and designed the dress herself for her wedding at Newtonmore on 5 July 1966. The dress, in French machine embroidered satin with a rich floral motif in gold and cream floss silk thread, is a simple sheath shape with a boat neckline and a bow on the waistband in typical 1960s style. The edge-to-edge coat is a fine cotton machine lace, with looped ribbon applied all over the surface. The bride also made her hat from artificial flowers and leaves in shades of pink, cream and white, with coarse net veiling. Her shoes were cream lace and mushroom suede with high stiletto heels and pointed toes.

Flower Power

1960s styles for bridesmaids also reflected the interest in romantic revivals and nostalgia. Simple loose posies of white daisies echoed the 'peasant' theme, while more formal bouquets in lace collars were reminiscent of Victorian arrangements. Flower balls were particularly popular, often carried by very young bridesmaids and attached to their wrists by ribbons chosen to tone with their dresses.

The photograph of the four-year-old bridesmaid was taken at a wedding in the Midlands in 1963. Following the adult fashion of

the time, she is wearing a heavy white satin dress finished with a broad pink sash that matched her 'grown-up' coiffure. She carries a small posy encircled by a stiff collar.

The two bridesmaids were attendants of Julia Harris at her wedding in 1964 (previous pages). Like the bride, they are dressed in empire line style, in hyacinth blue satin with a jacquard pattern. Their bouquets were made up in shades of cream and blue to compliment the dresses.

The third photograph was taken in Devon in 1967, and shows both modern and traditional wedding outfits. The three young bridesmaids wear full-length dresses and carry flower baskets, just like their Victorian predecessors. The page-boy has a ruffled shirt and tartan kilt. These costumes contrast strongly with the dress of the older girl, sister of the bride. Instead of a hat, she sports a very modern hairstyle, known as a 'Grecian perm'. Her short culotte suit in black crêpe came from Alastair Cowin in trendy Kensington Church Street in London, and the boots from the fashionable shoemakers, Eliot.

Twenty years later she recalled that her outfit shocked and upset everyone and they still teased her about it.

Select bibliography

Books

ARCH, Nigel and MARSCHNER, Joanna, *The Royal Wedding Dresses* (Sidgwick and Jackson, 1990)

ASHELFORD, Jane, *The Art of Dress* (The National Trust, 1996)

BAKER, Margaret, *Wedding Customs and Folklore* (David and Charles, 1977)

BRADFIELD, Nancy, *Costume in Detail 1730-1930* (George G. Harrap and Co., 1968)

BLACKER, Mary Rose, *Flora Domestica* (The National Trust, 2000)

BULLOCK, Charles, *Wedding Bells and Royal Weddings* (Home Words, n.d.c.1893)

CHARSLEY, Simon I., *Wedding Cakes and Cultural History* (Routledge, 1992)

CONEY, Sandra, *I Do, 125 years of Weddings in New Zealand* (Hodder Moa Beckett, Auckland, 1995)

CUNNINGTON, Phillis and LUCAS, Catherine, *Costume for Births, Marriages and Deaths* (A&C Black, 1972)

DAY, Ivan, 'Bridecup and Cake', in *Food and the Rites of Passage*, edited by Laura Mason (Prospect Books, 2002)

GINSBURG, Madeleine, *Wedding Dress 1740-1970* (HMSO, 1981)

HART, Avril and NORTH, Susan, *Historical Fashion in Detail: The 17th and 18th centuries* (V&A Publications, 1998)

HARTNELL, Norman, *Silver and Gold* (Evans Brothers, 1955)

HUMPHRY, Mrs, *Manners for Women* (1897, Reprinted in facsimile by Mapp and Bower, 1979)

JARVIS, Anthea, *Brides, Wedding Clothes and Customs, 1850-1980* (Merseyside County Museums, 1983)

JEAFFRESON, J.C., *Brides and Bridals* (two volumes, Hurst and Blackett, London, 1873)

JOHNSON, Mrs, *Bridesmaid and Bride* (Home Words Publications, 1893)

LANSDELL, Avril, *Wedding Fashions 1860-1980: Wedding Dress in Photographs* (Shire Publications, 1983)

LUCHETTI, Cathy, *I Do! Courtship, Love and Marriage on the American Frontier 1715-1915* (Crown, New York, 1996)

MONTSERRAT, Ann, *And the Bride Wore…The Story of the White Wedding* (Gentry Books, 1973)

PROBERT, Christina, *Brides in Vogue since 1910* (Thames and Hudson, 1984)

STANILAND, Kay, *In Royal Fashion, The Clothes of Princess Charlotte of Wales and Queen Victoria 1796-1901* (Museum of London, 1997)

STEVENSON, Pauline, *Bridal Fashions* (Ian Allen, 1978)

TOBIN, Shelley, *Inside Out* (The National Trust, 2000)

Articles

BAKER, Audrey, 'Wedding Bouquets', *Costume: The Journal of the Costume Society*, Number 6, 1972

BRADFIELD, Nancy, 'A wedding pelisse of 1814', *Costume: The Journal of the Costume Society*, Number 7, 1972

GINSBURG, Madeleine, 'Ladies' Court Dress: Economy and Magnificence', *The V&A Album*, No. 5, 1986

MARSHALL, Rosalind K, 'Three Scottish Brides', *Costume: The Journal of the Costume Society*, Number 8, 1974

STANILAND, Kay and LEVEY, Santina, ' Queen Victoria's Wedding Dress and Lace', *Costume: The Journal of the Costume Society*, Number 17, 1983

Exhibition catalogues and museum guidebooks
EDINBURGH, The Royal Scottish Museum, 'The Bride in her Time: Wedding Dresses from 1766 to 1945' (1980)

EXETER, Rougemont House Museum of Costume and Lace, 'Wedding Belles', (Exeter Museums Service, 1988)

MANCHESTER, Gallery of English Costume, Platt Hall, 'Weddings, Wedding Costume, 1735-1970', Picture Book Number 10 (Manchester City Art Gallery, 1976)

STOKE-ON-TRENT, 'For Better or for Worse, Wedding dresses from the museum collection' (The City Art Gallery and Museum, 1982)

Unpublished
TOBIN, Shelley, 'Charlotte Treadwin, Honiton Point Lace Manufacturer to Queen Victoria', (M.A. thesis, Winchester School of Art, University of Southampton, 1996)

Selection of contemporary magazines
A variety have been consulted including:
Brides (1956-)
Home Notes (1890-)
Roma's Pictorial Fashions
Weldons

Paris Fashions incorporating La Nouvelle Mode
Queen (1861-1971)
Family Friend
Girl's Own Paper
Illustrated London News (1834-)
Lady
Lady's Realm
Lady's Companion
Englishwoman's Domestic Magazine
Housewife
La Belle Assemblée
World of Fashion
Vogue (1914-)

For further information about magazines see:
WHITE, Christine, *Women's Magazines 1693-1968* (Michael Joseph, 1970)

List of Plates

The authors and publishers would like to acknowledge the institutions and individuals who have granted permission to reproduce their material in these pages.

Index